RESILIENCE
—AFTER—
GREAT LOSS

*Learning to Live & Grieve
Simultaneously*

ESLANA LOWER

Praise for *Resilience After Great Loss*

'Brilliant and raw. I wish this book was written long before now! What a gift for anyone that has or is experiencing grief or loss. This book gives us a whole new approach to the way we have been conditioned to grieve. A must read!'

– Corynne Woodger

'I read this beautifully written book in one sitting. As heartbreaking as it was in parts, I found myself smiling through tears and being quite inspired throughout.

Eslana's story challenged my original thoughts about grief and processing the unimaginable pain that we'll all experience in some form in our lifetime and I'm grateful for the new found perspective. Eye opening and just beautifully heartfelt storytelling.'

– Bec Purcell

Resilience After Great Loss: Learning to Live and Grieve Simultaneously
Published in Australia by Aila Media

First Edition
Copyright © Eslana Lower 2025

All rights reserved. No part of this book may be reproduced, stored in a retrieval system, or transmitted in any form or by any means—electronic, mechanical, photocopying, recording, or otherwise—without the prior written permission of the publisher, except in the case of brief quotations used in reviews or articles.

ISBN: #978-1-7642805-0-1 (paperback)
ISBN: #978-1-7642805-2-5 (epub)

Typeset by Kim Elliott

Every effort has been made to ensure the accuracy of the information contained in this book; however, the author and publisher accept no responsibility for any loss, damage, or injury that may result from the use or misinterpretation of this material. Contact details and resources were accurate at the time of publication but are subject to change. The advice and experiences shared are personal in nature and not a substitute for professional guidance. Readers are encouraged to seek professional support tailored to their individual circumstances.

 A catalogue record for this book is available from the National Library of Australia

National Library of Australia Cataloguing-in-Publication entry
Lower, Eslana.
Resilience after great loss: learning to live and grieve simultaneously / Eslana Lower.
ISBN: 978-1-922345-67-8 (paperback)
Subjects: Grief. | Resilience (Personality trait). | Loss (Psychology). | Self-help techniques. Dewey Number: 155.937 First edition, 2025

**Never in my wildest dreams did I imagine
I would be writing this book.**

*To my darling Rylee, you taught me about a love I would
never have known if not for the opportunity to be your mum—
thank you! I am eternally grateful to love you
and have been loved by you.*

*To the rest of my beautiful tribe—Jade, Mia, and Zali—
thank you also for the opportunity to be your mum;
to love you and be loved by you.*

*And for the love and self-love that each of you has also
taught me about in life. I will be forever grateful.*

I love you all endlessly.

Contents

11	**Foreword**
15	**Introduction**
19	**Impermanence**
19	*Rylee*
25	*The year that broke our hearts*
27	*Our grief is a wrecking ball*
30	*Whatever can happen at any time, can happen today*
32	*Welcome to anxiety*
39	**The Power of Mindset**
39	*The Kindness Crew*
50	*Grief is like the ocean*
52	*Why mindset matters*
57	*Hate is an expensive emotion*
69	**Resilience**
69	*I said yes to grief*
81	*Resilience through gratitude*
86	*Use gratitude like an insurance policy*
88	*How to make friends with gratitude in the thick of grief*
91	*The daily practice we didn't know would be our life raft*
96	*Gratitude is NOT the same as toxic positivity*
101	*Life is happening for me, not to me*
103	*Perception is like heads or tails–but YOU get to choose*
110	*Taming the ego*

117	**What Is Happiness?**
117	*What is happiness vs what it's not*
120	*Comparison is the thief of joy*
131	*Victim mentality serves no one*

143	**It's Okay To NOT Be Okay**
143	*I might be happy, but I'm not always okay*
156	*It's okay to say no in grief*
168	*Learning to live and grieve simultaneously*

175	**Love Letters & The Afterlife**
175	*A love letter to my inner child*
179	*A love letter to my daughter Rylee on her 12th birthday*
182	*Rylee and the butterflies*
197	*Ayahauasca and the afterlife*

205	**Complex Bereavement**
205	*A note on complex bereavement*

211	**Main Character Energy**
211	*Honouring my Main Character Energy*
221	*Reclaiming our Main Character Energy*
224	*Grief's martyrdom trap*

229	**About the Author**
231	*Useful Contacts*
232	*References*

Foreword

Grief is one of the few human experiences that unites us all. It does not only arrive with death. We grieve the end of relationships, the loss of health, the closing of chapters we once thought would last forever. Whether it comes suddenly or after a long goodbye, loss reshapes the way we see the world—and ourselves.

Yet, for most of us, we are not taught how to carry it. We are told to 'move on', 'stay strong', or that 'it will get easier'. But those who have lived with loss learn quickly: it does not simply get easier, no matter how much time passes. Instead, we learn how to live with it—how to weave grief into our days, allowing it to exist alongside love, joy, and even hope.

That is why this book matters. *Resilience After Great Loss* is not simply about survival; it is about the extraordinary courage to live and grieve at the same time. Eslana writes from a place few dare to go—with raw truth, tenderness, and unwavering love. Her words do not offer quick fixes or simple reassurances, but instead gently remind us that grief is different for everyone, there is no single path through it, and that grief and joy can coexist in the same heart.

What you hold in your hands is more than a book. It is a guide, a companion, and a testament to our ability to bend without breaking. Whether you are walking through the darkness of loss right now, or gently preparing yourself for life's storms, you will find in these pages both comfort and courage.

As you read, may you discover what Eslana so beautifully embodies: that the presence of grief does not erase joy, that love does not end with loss, and that resilience is not about forgetting–but about remembering with grace.

Because grief never leaves us. What changes is our ability to live fully while carrying it. Be gentle with yourself, and remember that grief brings up all forms of emotions–sometimes you may even feel lost–and that too is part of learning to live with loss.

– Maddy Suselj, Founder & Director of Believe In U

METAMORPHOSIS

There is something burning inside of me, and I write to release it.

What good am I if within me exists an empathy, knowledge and emotional intelligence—borne of firsthand experience of love, loss, tragedy and trauma—that is unable to escape as the butterfly it was determined to morph into?

It feels the same way I imagine the caterpillar does at the point in time its growth and transformation has resulted in too much pressure for the cocoon to withstand a moment longer, and so the butterfly must emerge.

Otherwise, what has it all been for?

Nothing? It can't be!

The courage it takes the caterpillar to withstand and endure all it must in order to be able to know the beauty of its wings and the freedom of flight.

You don't do all of that only to give up right before yielding the fruits of one's labour.

Introduction

If you're holding this book–or listening to these words–there's a good chance your life has been altered in a way you never imagined. Maybe you're standing in the thick fog of fresh loss. Maybe you're supporting someone through their own challenges. Or maybe life hasn't come for you yet, but something in your soul knows it will, one day.

> Wherever you are, I want to begin by saying, *I'm so sorry,* and *I'm so glad you're here.*

This book was not written from a place of healing, but from the raw, messy middle of survival. In 2022, I lost my 15-year-old daughter Rylee to suicide. There are no words that fully hold the weight of what that kind of loss does to a person. It shattered me. It reshaped me. And it forced me to learn how to live again in a world that would never be the same.

Grief like that doesn't end. It evolves. And what I discovered in the depths of that darkness was that it's absolutely possible to live and grieve simultaneously. Not to *move on*, but to *move forward* with meaning. Not to forget, but to remember in a way that makes life worth loving again.

This book is both my story and a survival guide. It's for anyone who needs permission to feel, to fall apart, to begin again. It's not filled with false hope or platitudes. It won't tell you to 'stay positive'. What it will do is meet you where you are with honesty, grace, and a fierce belief in your ability to keep going.

I'll share the tools and truths that helped me begin again—practices rooted in my GRACE framework, stories of resilience from the edges of despair, and the quiet, radical power of gratitude. Gratitude, for me, became less of a feeling and more of a lifeline. A kind of emotional insurance policy I had built over time without knowing I'd need it so much.

When the worst happened, gratitude didn't erase the pain—what it did do was soften the edges. It reminded me who I was beneath the heartbreak. You don't need to be strong all the time. You don't need to be ready. You just need to be willing to feel what's real, to open to the possibility of joy again, to live alongside your loss instead of in battle with it.

This is your invitation.

To honour your grief.

To reclaim your life.

To remember that resilience is not about bouncing back. It's about becoming someone new in the aftermath and finding beauty in the becoming.

Impermanence

Rylee

Following a childhood defined by poverty, neglect, trauma, physical, and sexual abuse that started for me at just 5 years of age, I left home at age 15 in an attempt to escape what I knew, even at that young age, did not serve me. Unfortunately, my late teens saw a continuation of abuse and trauma when I was drugged and date raped, followed by another sexual assault, another attempted sexual assault, stalked and then found myself in a DV relationship, much like that of my childhood home. The abuse in that relationship included psychological, emotional, financial, physical and sexual abuse, manipulation and control. Although this was all I had known at the hands of males, I desired more and deep down believed that it was possible.

My firstborn was a boy—Jade—when I was only 20 years old. I so badly wanted a son and will forever be grateful for the kindness life provided by allowing me to orientate myself to motherhood with a boy. You see, I truly and wholeheartedly believed I was meant to be the mother of boys. I felt too rough around the edges and ill-prepared to parent girls, and there was no foreseeable reality (in my mind) that included daughters. If I delved deeper, it would reveal that the true reason for my denial of this was pain and fear. I was angry—to the core. Anger was my best friend. It was my only friend and served to keep me safe by keeping others at bay. I thought I was assertive, but it turns out assertive and aggressive are not the same thing. I was so angry at life for being so unkind to me and in ways I never deserved. I had spent my entire life in fight or flight, revving the fuck out of my engine. It was like I had this angry, hurt and scared 5-year-old at the wheel of my life, and she was just running people over in an attempt to keep herself from being hurt again.

Life had definitely been a fight. For safety. For decency. For the bare minimum. So I was always ready. Ready and willing to fight. Fuelled by an anger that internally bordered on rage, or at the very least could seemingly so easily switch to. But my anger hadn't been easy to come by at all. It was fuelled by a lifetime of injustices that should never have happened and that subsequently made me so fearful of the responsibility of protecting daughters that, if it were up to me, I would 100 times over have chosen to be the mother of boys and only boys.

Fast forward to me meeting Ky, the man who would become my husband and father to the rest of my children. We lost our first baby at 12 weeks after I was in a minor car accident. Back then, nobody validated the grief and loss associated with early pregnancy loss. But for us, nothing about that pregnancy felt early! It's not just the 12 long weeks of waiting to see if the pregnancy is healthy or getting through the morning sickness and fatigue, or the fact that you've started telling people. It's the fantasising since you were little about the family you'd have and the fantasising since you became pregnant about the future, who they will be, what they will look like, what they will do with their life and how your life will be with them in it. It's the loss of all the unmet potential and love that will not get the opportunity to be expressed.

At the time, the hospital system was not designed to support our mental health following pregnancy loss, and once I was considered stable, we were discharged from the Emergency Department. As if we were just supposed to resume life as normal.

But nothing was normal. We lost our baby.

Men and women grieve differently. Miscarriage taught me that. Whilst I was emotional and hormonal–navigating loss while my body attempted to adjust itself to the absence of a life it had, until then been sustaining; he felt the need to be okay–for me. But this stoic approach came across (to me at least) as if he didn't care. As if he was just ok about it all. No support or counselling had been offered. After all, 1 in 4 pregnancies at the time ended in miscarriage, so I guess they and we just assumed people would just get on with it. The misunderstandings that arose from our differing grieving processes created distance and resentment, nearly ruining our relationship. Fortunately, we were emotionally intelligent and invested enough in our relationship to seek help in the form of relationship counselling. We learnt to communicate more effectively, and it helped us understand ourselves and each other better.

We fell pregnant again and I was so convinced (or rather in denial of any other possibility) that it was a boy. I was so devastated when there was no penis on the ultrasound. I cried for four weeks saying to Ky, *What am I going to do with a girl!* It makes me emotional to this day, remembering how visceral the fear felt.

I was so petrified of the responsibility of having and protecting a daughter. If my own mother couldn't do it, how on earth could I? Growing up, my mother never had the hard or confronting conversations about anything. Not periods and what to expect, sex, boys, drugs, any of it. It made me feel and believe that these types of conversations are clearly so hard to have that even parents can't have them. The absence of preparation that these conversations would've facilitated resulted in so much unnecessary and otherwise avoidable trauma across the years. And then so much shame, guilt, regret and remorse for me as a young woman, especially related to sex and my body. I didn't want that for a child, and therefore I didn't want daughters.

God knows parenting doesn't come with a rulebook and can often feel like you got the lead in a play and the spotlights on you, but no one gave you the lines... and at the end of the show you're probably going to be punished for getting the lines wrong... You know... the lines no one gave you!? And although we do the best we can with what we know, I knew very little other than how incredibly unkind and unsafe this world can be for a girl, even from a young age.

Fast forward again, and the next two babies we had were also girls. It's so egotistical to think we can plan life. We can have intentions... like to have children, but other than using IVF to gender select, then we need to accept that life has its own plan for us. As it turns out... a much wiser one than mine. You see, each one of them softened me more and more and showed me a love I would never have known if not for the opportunity to mother daughters.

Rylee, our firstborn daughter, was exactly that... love! From the moment she arrived. I would always describe her as our honeymoon love personified as 'Rylee'. When she was little, she was nicknamed *Smiley Rylee*.

She was just love.

It was confronting raising her as she was the most like me, and Ky would often say, 'She's like you... before the world got its hands on you'. The hardest part for me was the anger that came to the surface at the realisation that it really isn't that hard to love and protect a child. I needn't have worried. I was more than equipped to love this child. To protect her and even to have all of the age-appropriate 'hard conversations'. They really weren't hard at all. When everything comes from a conscious and intentional place of honesty and love and is directed at helping this little soul make sense out of the world around them, it's actually a privilege and not the scary chore I thought it would be. I loved loving Rylee and being loved by her. I loved seeing myself through her eyes. One day when she was about 8yrs old we were somewhere and she was sitting with her dad and as she watched me come into the room she tilted her head to the side and said with such love and admiration (about me) 'She's just so confident. She walks in with her shoulders back and her head high!'

She helped me learn to love and appreciate parts of myself that I wouldn't have seen without her. Everyone deserves a 'Rylee' in their life.

In 2022, we lost our 15-year-old daughter Rylee to bullying, which feels INSANE to write because it feels like yesterday I held her for the first time, and she was everything I didn't know I needed in my life. She was love, and my god, she loved me. We did everything we could to raise good humans! And then lost everything because others couldn't just *be kind*.

I had always said I don't believe our children are ours to control or make conform. I believe they are on loan to us to help prepare for the world so that we can release well-adjusted young adults into the world, who we can trust to make their own choices. And in doing so, not feel the need to control them as young adults. If I had known Rylee was only on loan to me for 15 years, I wouldn't have done anything differently… I loved her with every fibre of my being, and she knew that!

The year that broke our hearts

We lost our teenage daughter. A sentence I never thought I would have to say, but one that unfortunately and heartbreakingly became a part of our story in 2022.

I naively believed that conscious parenting and being open, honest and invested in my relationship with and to my children would mean that I would be able to prepare and protect them for/from the cruelties of the world in a way that would see them arrive safely at adulthood–reasonably unscathed and at the same time well-adjusted. You absolutely can do all of these things, and they should result in this. However, there was more my darling daughter was battling with than we were aware of, and bullying unravelled the effects of years of positive parenting in what seemed like a moment.

Then she was gone. Rylee took her life.

I also naively believed that staying on the 'right' side of the caring profession and healthcare system would somehow buffer and protect me from what has since proven to be the simultaneous savagery and intimacy of death and the loss of a loved one. Not just a loved one—my baby!

Working in Emergency, ICU and even Midwifery will quickly teach you that tragedy and loss may be waiting around any corner, and to live without regret because tomorrow is definitely NOT promised to anyone. Life may teach it, but no matter how good a student of life we may think we are, we only learn it in theory, on a relatively superficial level, until life decides to come for you, that is. Until it is your turn to learn, truly learn, about the kind of grief, loss and pain that arrives in a way that makes everything you thought you knew about these three topics pale in comparison to the gut-wrenching, soul-crushing agony that is the loss of your child.

Never in my wildest dreams could I have imagined it would be my child. Seems egotistical now... to think that by caring for others, holding space for and supporting them in and through their grief would somehow shield me from the same or similar life experiences. What makes it worse is that my life was mostly lived in a relative sense of isolation aimed at limiting my exposure to loss. After a childhood of abuse, trauma and neglect, I subconsciously assumed that by limiting the number of those I let close to me, I would in turn, protect myself from, not only further harm in life, but also from loss. All this did was limit my exposure to the kinds of losses I think are supposed to, in a sense, 'break you in' when it comes to grief and loss.

After all, you cannot love and not experience loss.

You cannot even live without avoiding loss. I now know firsthand how relative and bittersweet the fact is that the sense of loss experienced is directly related to the degree of love shared.

Our grief is a wrecking ball

My ex-husband and I trauma-bonded following the loss of our eldest daughter in a way that I believe was absolutely necessary (initially) in order for all of us to survive. I cannot imagine trying to navigate the first couple of years of grief had we lived on separate properties, and in doing so would have been without our surviving children (and even each other) for periods of time as they went between homes. We ended up purchasing a property that had two homes on it so that we could finish raising our children as neighbours and choose kindness. This allowed all of us the time and space to heal sufficiently enough that we would reach a point where moving on felt not only possible but necessary.

Our experience of grief in the early days was like a wrecking ball... swinging between us. Sometimes it collides with you and you stumble, trying desperately to regain your emotional footing so that you can continue to be everything you need to be... for yourself, each other and your surviving children.

Other times it hits so hard, knocking you for 6 and leaving you feeling completely overwhelmed and wondering how on earth you will possibly manage to make it back to your feet. Let alone keep putting one foot in front of the other if you do manage to (like everyone keeps reminding you you must).

BUT it is a wrecking ball. And wrecking balls don't swing in more than one direction at a time. So whilst one of us is down, fortunately, the other not so much. Yes... The other may still be stumbling back to their feet. But at least not both are being hit with the same force, at the same time. We have been able to bring awareness to this and not only appreciate the times when we feel (albeit slightly) more solid in our footing, allowing us to hold space for the other whilst remembering that our turn for next impact is likely not far off and most certainly likely to happen when we least expect it.

That's the thing about PTSD, and the anxiety that has subsequently taken up residence at the base camp of our soul is... You just don't know when it is going to decide to invade your psyche and ruin your day.

Learning to live with a crippling anxiety that will see you self-isolate and inevitably steal your sanity if you are not self-aware (and invested in working with an appropriately trained grief, trauma and loss therapist) became one of life's many newfound challenges. The irony of what ruins others' day becomes apparent as you find yourself feeling sorry for people who think bad traffic, a shitty coffee or someone being rude is the worst thing that could've happened.

Clearly, life has not yet 'come for them'! Pity becomes all you can muster as you leave these interactions thinking, 'if only they knew how good they had it...?'.

Oh, how I would give anything to be disgruntled over a shitty coffee!

Whatever can happen at any time, can happen today

At approximately 9:45pm, on the 17th of November 2022, our world came to a horrifically traumatic halt. The world has never spun so fast around us. Yet we were stuck. Halted by the unimaginable. Rylee jumped off my balcony, 33 stories high, with me and her sisters home, and I had to go down and find her. The girls who were aged 11 years and 13 years at the time heard my screams from 33 stories up, so they came down (and saw her body on the ground surrounded by broken glass).

The screams that left my body were a sound I was all too familiar with from my years in emergency, and the same sound every parent made when they found out their child had passed.

But I didn't 'find out'. *I was there.* No one told me. It's forever imprinted in my mind's eye as a type of Groundhog Day I've relived every night since.

It was an excruciating guttural agony in the form of a sound. The mix of a torturous ache combined with disbelief, fear, sorrow and the pain of heartache. Life-shattering heartache! Something I had thought I'd known in life, but that in that moment awakened in me a knowing that everything we'd considered to be pain and suffering prior would now pale in comparison to what had come to claim my soul that night.

Never in my wildest dreams could I have imagined I would lose a child. Let alone in such a horrifically traumatic way. In an instant, my heart felt forever shattered, and my spirit completely broken as every day was now some kind of cruel existence where survival felt like life's primary goal.

Every cell in my body ached with a longing to end the pain I didn't know my child felt was all-consuming and so much that in her mind the only option was to leave this life... without warning or explanation!? My soul was shattered in an instant, and my heart broken beyond repair. Happiness no longer felt attainable or realistic, and any experience resembling fun was met with a renewed and overwhelming sense of pain and guilt as life whispered... 'How dare you!?'

I felt as though I was dying a slow death of a broken heart, only to wake up each new day and face the same slow death.

The human connection necessary for survival seems overwhelmingly as though it is a double-edged sword of value vs vulnerability. Love, connection and friendship are of undeniable value, but at the same time expose our vulnerability at predisposing ourselves to further loss and grief in life by allowing said love, connection and friendship. Agreed, the chance of loss is not reason enough to avoid love, connection and friendship, BUT the grief associated with the loss of a child is so heavy that the thought of any further losses feels unsurvivable.

And (if I'm lucky) I'm only halfway through my life!? How am I supposed to survive the inevitable losses that come with living and ageing... especially if I don't know how to survive this unimaginable loss and the associated agonising heartache that accompanies it?

Welcome to anxiety

Born in the 80's I always thought 'anxiety' was a kind of label people used... some kind of excuse. I didn't mean to have this perception; it's just how I was raised. After all, we didn't have the luxury of labels or excuses. We had parents with a mentality of 'did you die?' and 'suck it up.' You just had to get on with life, despite the challenges that would break most people and that we now realise as unacceptable, controlling, manipulative and abusive.

Experiencing the sudden, unexpected and horrifically traumatic suicide of my 15-year-old daughter resulted in Complex PTSD, which brings with it my newfound friend *Anxiety*.

Turns out I was wrong. Very wrong!

Anxiety is NOT a label nor an excuse.

It's an unwelcome squatter that takes up residence in your soul and visits when you least expect it and definitely don't want it.

For the longest time, I would find myself worrying that my mind was betraying me. Letting the intensity of my existence slip from memory like grains of sand through one's fingertips. Grief compounding this, seemingly speeding up the rate at which I fade into the darkness that's become my mind. And grief having wiped the hard drive of my memory, which seems no longer able to recognise the value or significance of retaining day-to-day necessities.

Is this what I am now? A shell of what was. Unsure of what will be. But witness to my own demise as I watch my brain fail to cope with the heaviness of grief in a way that makes retaining information seemingly impossible.

Am I to spend my remaining days apologising for my memory? Yet worrying that maybe this is more than grief... more than trauma? What if this is life's cruel sequel and I AM actually dying... albeit slowly... but dying all the same!?

Welcome to ANXIETY.

I found myself unable to retain simple information, names, faces, or anything that had happened prior to her death. If asked something that required my mind to search back into the archives of my memory, it would land on her death. I would find myself standing there, not only unable to answer, but as I was reliving the memory, only able to muster the phrase 'I'm not sure, sorry... my daughter died'. This is a weird response to a question like 'Oh you're a Nurse, did you ever work with Susan?' The alternative would be someone who approaches me smiling as if I should know them and as they start talking my PTSD interrupts with the 'I'm sorry I know I should know who you are but my daughter died...'

I think (at least in this case) it is not just a symptom of trauma but perhaps one of the brain's many ways of coping with and even protecting itself in the aftermath. My brain knew that, at least for a period, I really couldn't deal with more. So anxiety made me avoid so many things. I guess in an attempt to mitigate the risk of further trauma. Unfortunately, anxiety feels a lot like having a small child at the wheel of your life, trying to make decisions about your safety and what serves you. Obviously, a small child would not be best equipped or capable of making the right decisions.

People say time heals.

People say all kinds of things.

What it actually does is allow the repeated exposure to their absence; which is required in order for the brain to move from denial to a more conscious reconciliation of their absence as permanent and the realisation that life is worth living - despite its fragility and suffering.

Some people choose denial in different forms and in doing so (perhaps subconsciously) prolong it. But it's the willingness and ability to lean into each painful reminder and to experience the inevitable waves of grief and emotional overwhelm that, in time, lessen the crippling effects that hold you back from living.

Don't get me wrong- grief will continue to come in waves, some that momentarily grab you right in the chest, stealing your breath and overwhelming you with disbelief that this is, in fact, your reality. Other times, it will make getting through the day feel like an insurmountable feat. In time, you begin to find the ability to lean into and allow, if not validate, each of these states of being with empathy and self compassion, moving gentler through life as they occur, and not expecting too much from yourself whilst knowing that this too shall pass (not the grief but the intensity of its visit).

* Fortunately, in time and with conscious and concerted effort in taking back the driver's seat of my journey through both therapy and adapting my life to suit what it has and is becoming, (rather than trying to make it fit what it was or perhaps what I think it should be) meant that I have been able to get to a place where anxiety is no longer a part of my journey.

Impermanence

There is no permanence. Learn to embrace it rather than resist.

Everything in life is a lesson or a gift. Sometimes both.

Nothing lasts—it's a blessing, not a curse.

Use this knowledge. Learn life's lessons.

Live now.

Love hard.

Be honest.

And authentic.

Choose kindness.

And always... ALWAYS make sure those you love know you do.

Weather life's storms with courage.

Find gratitude in and for everything.

Trust that everything softens with time,

even the sharp edges of grief.

And the tears that remain are the unexpressed love seeping, through the scars left behind by the impermanence of life.

The same scars that were once wounds you swore would never heal,

yet sewn together at the edges by love, courage, gratitude and kindness.

They form a scar that remains not to punish you,

but rather as a reminder of a love so strong it left its mark

in a world where impermanence is guaranteed.

The Power of Mindset

The Kindness Crew

Pretty early in our grief, the girls came to me saying they wanted to start a business. Zali had just turned 12, and Mia was nearly 14 at this time. My initial thought was 'Far out! I'm trying to keep *my* business afloat!'

As if I needed to be helping launch a new business! I kind of fobbed them off, suggesting they look into drop shipping, as that would mean they could make money but without getting their hands dirty, so to speak.

The motivation behind their ongoing requests was that they realised that life is short and wanted to travel, but didn't want me to have to pay for it. Initially, I thought it was just an attempt to distract themselves from their newfound reality and the aftereffects of our trauma, but it was more than that. They saw how hard life already was for me, juggling grief, immeasurable loss, trauma and trying to run a business. They didn't want to burden me with the added financial pressure of paying, but they also didn't want to miss out on the travel and adventure they truly desired, because they didn't have jobs to pay for themselves. They were trying to take things into their own hands and believed that they could make it happen.

They then came to me with their business name ideas, their logos made, and their online cart (ready to go) with everything they needed to get started. How do you say no to that!? So began what would prove to be quite the adventure. Initially, Mia was making handmade earrings and called her business 'Made by Mia', and Zali was making handmade bracelets that said 'BE KIND' and called herself 'Bracelets by Zali'. The school got behind them by offering them a stall at the PBC weekend markets. We found t-shirts that said 'Be Kind' and headed off for the markets. Looking back, the time-consuming nature of making all the jewellery ended up being such a beautifully valuable way to positively pass the time in those early days of our grief.

Their first day at the markets, we had to get up at 4.30am to get there and get the stall set up before they officially opened. The weather was so cold you could see your breath. I looked at both girls, who, whilst understandably cold, did not look at all inviting and asked, 'Are you girls happy to be here?' To which they both enthusiastically replied, 'Yeah, of course!' I said, 'Then tell your face! Cos your shirt says BE KIND but your face says fck off!'

They giggled knowingly. Although said in jest, I explained to the girls that you never know just how much a simple smile could mean to someone and the importance of being aware not to have a resting bitch face when you are in frontline customer service.

The morning went well, and their stall was well-received. About 11am, an American gentleman came marching over to Mia and said, 'What is your name?' She replied, 'Mia'. He said, smiling from ear to ear, 'Mia, the way you smiled at me and maintained eye contact!... Sell me something!' He introduced himself to Zali and went on to say how well he thought the girls would do in business before finalising his purchase and walking away. I chased him down to say thank you and explain that he had just reinforced what I had been trying to teach my girls. As we spoke, he realised I had tears running down my face he asked if I was okay. I explained that we had recently lost their sister to suicide because of bullying. He hugged me before offering to be a business mentor to the girls, and then offered Mia a babysitting job, saying he wanted her energy rubbing off on his 5-year-old daughter. Little did we know at the time, but we would become friends with this man and his family.

The girls did so well at the markets that day, but quickly realised that they needed to combine forces and focus on the 'Be Kind' bracelets rather than earrings, as the kids loved them so much. They morphed into one and called themselves 'The Kindness Crew'. The next week, they were a hit... Kids running up excitedly saying, 'We found you!' As they would pull out their pocket money to buy their kindness crew bracelet. The American gentleman then did a post on his social media explaining about these girls he'd met at the markets who had chosen kindness in their grief and how they were spreading a message of kindness, reinforcing that kindness is a choice - not always an easy one, BUT a very important one and one that could save lives.

As a result, the girls were inundated with orders from America and suddenly needed to make nearly 100 handmade 'Be Kind' bracelets. This was on top of what they needed to make for the markets. We couldn't keep up.

We ended up needing to source wristbands that we had made in rainbow colours (to honour Rylee) that said 'The Kindness Crew - CHOOSE KINDNESS'. They came in 4 sizes from tiny toddler to child, teen and adult. We also had some of the wristbands made into keyrings. The three of us would spend each evening making the bracelets as we watched movies or listened to music. I have such fond memories of nights that could easily have been spent feeling down or depressed, but instead were made joyful by how well received the girls' business had been.

After each market day, we would pack up and head off to a lunch date together. Taking our time to enjoy what was left of our Saturday, we would get home and eventually unpack, but I made sure to really take my time getting to the part where I would count their money. I liked that it was never about the money. They would be so happy to bring home stories about all the kids who were so excited to have found them and get their own kindness crew bracelet like their friends, that the joy of spreading kindness and love felt like payment enough. I love that they got to experience what it feels like to do something you are passionate about, and how it never feels like work when that is the case. Eventually, I would ask, 'Okay, how much do you think you made?' They would both guess, only to be overwhelmed when the actual amount was often twice what they had expected.

We made a website for people to purchase from (as the Americans were asking how they could order), and the girls would make each order up, then add a positive affirmation sticker and a hand-written thank you note to each order before posting them. They were sending orders to the states and all over Australia. We also had some business cards made that had a QR code to their website on one side and a brief explanation about Rylee's passing being the motivation to spread a message of kindness on the other side. This made the markets easier as I could just hand it to the parents instead of having to constantly repeat our story (which, although the girls didn't need to talk about it, I could tell my explaining it over and over was beginning to take its toll on all of us). Although the girls pre-made the bracelets, as children would come and find the pattern of beads/colours they liked, we would resize them on the spot for each individual. Each time we were at the markets, more kids would find us and say, 'OMG, it's the kindness crew! My friend has your bracelet! I came here just for you... I want one too!'

There is something very special about the joy that comes from not just choosing kindness but spreading it. The months we spent getting up early to head to the markets were incredibly therapeutic for the girls and gave them not only a sense of purpose but also something to look forward to.

During this time, I had met a man at a conference who was hosting an upcoming entrepreneurs' event on the Gold Coast, and when he learned about the girls and The Kindness Crew asked me to bring the girls with me to his event. He said that he wanted to bring them up on stage and that we should bring as many bracelets/wristbands as possible.

He met with them before the event started and explained to the girls what he intended to do. He said he wanted to make an example of them and that if they could do this at just 12 years and 14 years old, then there would probably be an adult or two in the audience who had been doubting themselves, but would feel more confident in taking the leap if they heard the girl's story. During the event, he invited us up on stage. He introduced the girls saying, 'This is Mia and

Zali, and they are selling these wristbands for $15 each that say 'Choose Kindness'. Who wants one?' A couple of people put their hands up. The girls looked at me nervously because we weren't selling them for $15! We had been selling them for $10 each or two for $15.

He then said, 'Okay, I want to tell you how I met their mum...' He went on to explain about how we had lost Rylee and that the girls had formed The Kindness Crew in an attempt to spread a message of kindness, reminding people that kindness is a choice. The 3 of us stood on the stage, staring at the floor as tears fell from our eyes and our arms around each other's waists. I looked up and saw nearly 300 people in tears. He said, 'Okay, now who wants one!?... For $50ea?' So many people jumped to their feet. He said, '$70 each!' Not one person sat down. He looked at the girls and said 'This is how even Tiffany and Co find their price point, you just keep going until people start to tap out' He said to the crowd, 'They also have these cool keyrings so if you want one they are $70 or you can get both for $100' That's when two people sat down. He told the crowd, 'You'll find the girls outside during the lunch break, you can grab your Kindness Crew bracelets there'. He thanked us and we left the stage, returning to our seats.

At lunch, we sat nervously on the lounges in the foyer. Almost immediately, there was a line-up of people wanting to purchase from the girls. The first man said, 'I'll take 3 sets please'. My hands shaking as I held the square reader for him to pay I asked 'How much did you want to pay?' He said with a smile 'Darling he said they were $100 a set, that's $300!' And promptly paid, congratulating the girls on forming such beautiful bond and delivering on such a great cause. They made $900 in 5min and $3000 that day.

What was of greatest value that day was the sense of community and connection they received, and the ability to show them that although there are plenty of unkind people in the world, there are so many more that are kind. It showed them the power of finding your tribe and that you really can achieve anything if you have a passion for it and surround yourself with people who want to see you succeed, as they will lift you by default.

The girls kept doing the markets and ended up travelling. For Zali's 13th birthday, we went to Bali. The girls paid for their own flights, part of the accomodation (they said at one of the places they would prefer to upgrade the room and offered to pay the extra $150 each to do so), they took their own spending money and although I thought I was paying for meals, they would sit down and look at the menu deciding on what to eat based on what they were willing to spend! They managed their money so well that they even brought a couple of hundred dollars home with them. It was invaluable - they learnt more about life, living, bartering, poverty, compassion, and handling money (including a foreign currency) in the two weeks they missed of school than they would in an entire year spent in any school classroom.

It was also the first proper holiday I had ever been on... I didn't take my children on holiday—I joined them on theirs!

They drank mocktails with drag queens and sang karaoke. All the super drunk Aussies in the karaoke bar thought the fact that these 13-year-old and nearly 15-year-old sisters picked American Pie by Don McLean was only trumped by the fact that they knew the words. They were like rock stars in the eyes of these overly intoxicated Australians. It was great! I've always loved that song (hence why the girls know it). Still, it will forever hold the fondest memories of an incredibly healing time spent with my girls in Bali, where they got to let their hair down, momentarily set their grief aside and truly just live the shit out of the two weeks spent adventuring.

Watching the local bartenders ply the tourists with alcohol until they didn't know where they were, then overcharge them on their bill hoping they were too intoxicated to notice, then witnessing a man drop his wallet, vomit in the street and then nearly get run over because he could barely walk taught them valuable lessons about the importance and merit of RSA (responsible service of alcohol) and why we have it in Australia.

Seeing the same tourists grossly hungover at the resort the following day also taught them valuable lessons about the effects of alcohol without having to partake and learn firsthand. They saw how easily the intoxicated can be harmed, injured and/or taken advantage of, and it facilitated conversations around how, when people live in poverty, it makes them act for survival in ways that don't always consider the implications of those actions, and how to travel safely, especially as a female.

Five weeks later, we went on our first-ever cruise ship for my birthday, and the girls contributed $1000 each toward the $6000 trip that saw them see Noumea and New Caledonia. They met so many other teens on the cruise and had what they still refer to as their 'best holiday ever'.

They eventually reached a point of emotional exhaustion, and in time, we ended up stepping back from the markets. They still, to this day, will be somewhere and see someone wearing a Kindness Crew wristband. We even had a man come up to us at the shops recently and say with a giant grin, 'Hey, you guys made that Be Kind bracelet for me at the markets!'

Knowing that Rylee had been bullied by someone who had previously been like family to us could've easily led any of us, including the girls, to do anything but choose kindness. They were aware that Snapchat had been used to bully Rylee, and in time, we even had discussions about what was said. I didn't bring it up to them, but as time went on, they naturally began asking questions. My endeavour as a parent was always to raise girls who would be honest with me, and I knew from an early age, that you don't get to the teenage years and then suddenly have a great, open and honest relationship with your children. It starts when they are young, with you providing age-appropriate honesty.

The truth was something I had always offered my girls. I never tried to sugarcoat it either. I would always give them honest answers. So when they started asking more about what had been said to Rylee, I was honest. Careful, but honest. I explained how I believed that Rylee keeping things to herself instead of discussing and unpacking them, negatively impacted her mental health so rapidly that I believe even if she had wanted to discuss any of it, she wouldn't have known where to start. I explained how no matter how big or small something seems, the child's mind is not usually mature enough to see it in the same light that an adult can; and that's why we are best equipped to help them navigate the challenges of life, but that we also don't know what we don't know. I answered their questions as they arose and offered them the same age-appropriate honesty I always had.

The most important thing is that they saw me choose kindness. They also saw it doesn't mean going out of your way to be kind to someone who has wronged you. It could be as simple as choosing kindness for yourself by removing yourself from a situation that doesn't serve you. It could also mean not holding onto anger that will not change the past or bring the person back. The Kindness Crew was their acknowledgement that kindness is, in fact, a choice and that we understand (better than most) that it is not always an easy one. It is, however, one of the most important choices you will make in almost all situations.

Whether or not to choose kindness.

It's a choice that is so important as it could actually save a life. We all crave connection. You never know what someone may be going through and just how powerful a simple act of kindness may be in impacting their journey.

Grief is like the ocean

I would liken my experience of grief to being in the ocean. Life prior to this kind of trauma and loss is a lot like being knee deep in the ocean and thinking, ' This is it! I'm in the ocean. I know what it means to be in the ocean.'

But it turns out our capacity for everything we know the human experience to be pales in comparison to the capacity we actually have to experience it all. Love, joy, happiness, sadness, anger, rage. We only actually know them all on a very superficial level. You see, post significant trauma and loss is like being deep in the ocean, so far out that the water looks almost black and is so deep you could never even attempt to swim to the bottom and survive.

Now you're in the ocean.

The waves crash around you, initially almost drowning you as each one hits. You barely catch your breath before another wave hits you, driving home the harsh reality that THIS is what it's like to be IN the ocean. And now that you are, you never get to return to the naive version of you; knee deep back at the shore, convinced you know what it means to experience the depths and vastness of this human experience we are referring to as the ocean, yet so very naive about the capacity we have to experience all of those emotions on such a level that is immensely overwhelming and at times almost too much for the human soul to bare.

Initially, you're convinced you couldn't possibly survive the overwhelming nature of the ocean's true force and depth. But you CAN survive! And do so at first, by finding something, anything to hold onto... anything. As a kind of flotation device. Then something more resembling a life raft and in time hopefully more of a beautiful yacht, surrounded by people who love you, but aware all the same that this is you now... out in the depths, never to return to the naive shores of knee deep and superficial.

I couldn't see it at first. For the longest time, I was convinced there would never be a yacht. That 'beautiful' and 'joyful' would never again have a place as adjectives associated with my existence. But I'm happy to tell you that that was just a lie grief tells you in an attempt to enslave you. Your mindset is what will facilitate that 'beautiful yacht' on which you absolutely can learn how to live (and grieve simultaneously) on, in your newfound reality that is the ocean.

Why mindset matters

Whilst we may find ourselves standing in the rumble of a life we no longer recognise and feeling as though we are on a foreign planet of which we no longer speak the native tongue, the good news is we can survive the unimaginable. We can even do better than survive... in time, as we learn to live and grieve simultaneously, we can thrive.

It is, after all, not the environmental factors of our life or what happens in and around it that determine our capacity for joy, happiness and contentment; but rather the lens through which we view it and what we do with the parts we can control.

This is why some people are miserable even in what appears to be the absence of significant loss or trauma, and why some will survive unimaginable challenges, coming through them better and even happier versions of themselves in the aftermath. The determinants aren't their circumstances, but rather their mindset and the lens through which they view their life!

For years (before losing Rylee) I taught workshops around mindset and how we can use emotional intelligence and and self awareness to be able to harness the power we (all) have to take accountability for the parts of our life we can control and change, and do so in a way that lends itself to rewarding outcomes despite any potential challenges or forks in the road.

After all, there isn't any area of your life where your mindset doesn't matter.

And I believe that we harness the power of our mindset by becoming consciously aware of our limiting beliefs, our internal narratives and subconscious defaults. And as we do, we will likely find that most are outdated and don't serve us and (whether positive or negative) ALL are impacting both our lived experience and our perception of it.

It's about living intentionally, creating a life by design, not by default, making sure that my mindset is aligned with my values and the kind of life that I want to live and not giving my power away - something we do daily, in ways we don't even realise we're doing.

I appreciate that talking about creating a life by design rather than default may sound weird in the aftermath of such significant and unimaginable trauma and loss, as I most certainly would not have included it in my life design or plan if given the choice. However, I want to clarify something. You having your best and most rewarding life experience has less to do with the environmental factors of how your life plays out and more to do with your response to them. It is NOT about controlling what happens, it's about controlling and being responsible for your actions, reactions and mindset.

Your mindset is the lens through which you view your life, your loss, your pain, your worth, your possibilities... the lens through which you view everything in your life.

EVERYTHING.

And if we are using or implementing one that doesn't serve us, improving our quality of life can be as simple as beginning to take accountability for what we as individuals can do to change that. We can't plan life, but we absolutely can plan for it... Then go about acting intentionally in a way that takes ownership over our journey. By understanding the difference and positioning ourselves to be able to act (and react) from a place of intention, we get to facilitate a lived experience that is far more rewarding than we might've imagined.

In the coming chapter, I speak about the power of gratitude and how we can use it as an insurance policy across the lifespan to be able to navigate the inevitable storms of life in a way that sees them be a kinder and softer version of that experience. By no means am I saying that by using the daily practice of gratitude, we will avoid the storms of life?

We won't avoid them. And by no means am I saying that by using the daily practice of gratitude, our storms will be kind and soft. Because let's be real, kind and soft is by definition the opposite of storms.

What I am saying is that they will be kinder and softer versions of them for us to experience. It doesn't mean that they'll be easy. It means that we will be more aware of the capacity we (all) have to be able to weather these storms in a way that facilitates learning to live and grieve simultaneously, and that maintains our ability to see this as a temporary state. As a storm, and that this too shall pass. And to be able to choose what I do with what happens in and around my life to inform me and the response that I have to each of those life events, whatever it may be.

Whilst I don't get to choose everything that happens in my life, I do get to choose my response, what I do with what happens and how I let that impact me as a person, how I carry myself through life and what I choose to do moving forward. Or whether I move forward at all?

Because how our life unfolds, how our trauma, our grief, how all these things that are part of the lived experience unfold, is not what will validate or nullify our capacity for contentment or happiness, but rather how we view and respond to all of these things and who we allow ourselves to become in response to them.

Our contractual agreement with this life is that we get to live, love, have passion, adventure, all of these things, but that the flip side is that we have to also accept that there will be an associated grief and sadness at the absence or loss of the very things we held nearest and cherished most. There are two sides to every coin, and I can't love as intensely as I do, so wholeheartedly and not experience the flip side of the coin, being grief at the absence of the thing or the person that I loved so deeply.

So if we accept that this is part of the lived experience, and we acknowledge that I'm not special, that unfortunately, I don't get to live out this life unscathed, and that in one way or another life is likely to come for me; we can begin to ask ourselves 'What am I going do about that to be able to carry myself through life in a way that sees me keep moving forward and not get stuck?'

I am definitely not saying that the whole experience of life is going to be exciting and rewarding or even fulfilling. If anything, I'm saying it won't!

I'm saying that regardless of the heaviness, the ugliness, the intensity of the challenges that you may be facing or will face, you are 100 % capable of facing them. You are 100 % capable of learning how to live and grieve simultaneously in a way that lends itself to a joy-filled existence. A joy that can coexist with grief.

As impossible as that might be to conceive right now if you're in the thick of it and you're standing in the rubble of a life you no longer even recognize, then I'm here to tell you the good news... no, great news... is that there are some things that you can do and responses that you can choose (to how you view life) that will facilitate a more positive experience of it and the chapters that follow will provide more detail.

Hate is an expensive emotion

In order to have a balanced and rewarding life, we need to stop giving our power away... to stop giving our power away, we need to have the courage to examine the ways we (might not even realise) we are doing it and have the willingness to change these behaviours.

Blame is one way we do this. When things go wrong, it's human nature to look to place blame or make someone accountable. We somehow think that if we find the why it happened or who caused it, that it will make things make sense and/or somehow lessen our pain. This is definitely not the case.

I understand this firsthand since my daughter took her life in large part because of bullying. We would later find out she was also being groomed by her lesbian supervisor, who had her convinced she was bisexual and, after 'coming out' to her friend group, was then maliciously bullied and encouraged to take her life by someone she had considered closest to her.

I say 'convinced she was bisexual' because prior to working with the groomer, Rylee had never shown any interest in girls. Throughout their childhood, I had regular check-ins with my girls about their sexuality in an attempt to normalise any sexual orientation and provide a safe space for their sexual orientation and/or exploration to land. Whenever I had asked questions like 'Do you think when you are ready, you will have a boyfriend or a girlfriend?' Rylee never waivered. She would just smile at me and say, 'Just a boyfriend, mum.'

We didn't learn any of this until months after her passing. After reviewing messages and voice recordings, it became clear that the bullying—both online while she was at home and in person at school—was frequent, targeted, and deeply harmful. It was also the conclusion of the police investigations into her unexpected passing that this ongoing behaviour had played a significant role in what happened.

Our emotions create our feelings, but they also influence our actions by affecting our nervous system. Whilst we are not responsible for every thought that pops into our heads, we are responsible for what we do with them. For example, I can acknowledge that someone contributed to her passing, but if I dwell on thoughts of blame, it can lead to strong emotions like anger or even rage. These emotions can disrupt our nervous system and may lead us to react in ways that don't align with who we are or who we want to be.

I understand firsthand the rage that is possible and that has the potential to lead anyone to homicide. ***Yes, even you!***

The thing is, we like to think we are different from those who harm people, and of course, we are... different from those who go about harming another for some kind of pleasure or enjoyment. The capability, however, to cause or even desire to harm another human is simply on the other side of enough pain. When you lose someone you were never meant to outlive, and then learn that another person deliberately caused them harm–and even escalated that harm when it became visible–it can awaken a level of rage you didn't know you were capable of feeling. In that state, thoughts of retaliation can feel overwhelming, and the line between thought and action can begin to blur.

At first, when I learned what had been happening to Rylee, I tried to let it go. I knew that focusing on the behaviours of others wouldn't bring her back. For a few days, I genuinely attempted to move forward without going down that path.

But something wouldn't let me rest.

I reached out to one of Rylee's close friends and asked, 'I'm not naming anyone, but was there someone who was giving Rylee a hard time?' Without hesitation, she named the person—and then began sending me screenshots and a voice message that revealed more than I could have ever imagined. What I heard and read were relentless and cruel attacks telling Rylee her life wasn't worth living, and that there was no place in the world for someone like her, because she had said she liked both boys and girls.

Heartbroken and unsure what to do, I contacted another parent for guidance. That's when she mentioned overhearing teens at Rylee's celebration of life say to the same individual, 'This is all your fault,' as they walked by.

It hit me that this young person—who had their own history of mental health struggles and previous suicide attempts—could now be in danger themselves, especially if they were being targeted because of their actions toward Rylee. Despite everything, I reached out to their parent. At first, the response was defensive, which I understood. I explained that I wasn't looking to place blame—I just didn't want anyone else to hurt like I did. I didn't want another family to go through what we were going through because no one warned them that their child was hurting. Even though this child's actions caused deep pain, I could never wish that level of suffering on anyone. No one deserves to hurt the way we do, the way we still do, and always will.

I later contacted the principal of their school to express concern that this student might be at risk of self-harm. Given the circumstances and their history, I felt it was essential that someone in a position of care was aware.

After speaking with both the parent and the school, a plan was formed—one that felt instinctively right at the time. The idea was for me to reach out to the student directly, as a way to extend care and possibly offer a form of forgiveness, or at least reassurance that I didn't want any more harm to come from what had already happened.

That afternoon, Ky and I walked to the beach and made the call. Surrounded by family support, the teen listened as I told them I didn't believe Rylee ever intended to hurt anyone—she simply wanted her pain to end. I asked them to delete anything negative that had passed between them and Rylee, and I offered to send a letter I had found on Rylee's phone—one she had written to this same person a year earlier. In it, she shared how much she valued their friendship and how deeply she cared for them.

I told them, 'If you're tempted to think about Rylee, this is how I want you to remember her.' Through tears, I tried to express what I believe with all my heart—that no matter how hard things get, there is nothing in life so bad that it's worth hurting yourself over.

I got off the phone and collapsed. *It was the hardest thing I had ever done.* Harder than Rylee's celebration of life.

Probably because her celebration of life was survived and endured in a state of shock and denial, and this event was the opposite. It was conscious and intentional. It felt completely necessary to not just potentially save this child's life and their family from the pain we were experiencing, but probably saved my life without me knowing it at the time. To reach out from a place of love (for Rylee) and forgiveness.

When I would tell people that the police kept her phone for 4 months and had deleted everything before returning it us their response was always, 'How could they do that?'. This was my initial response too. The only reason I knew about the bullying at all was because when I changed the face ID to mine for her recently deleted, there were still screenshots of the bullying conversations there. When I went back into her phone the following day, it had self-deleted. It was never their intention for me to know about the bullying.

Let me tell you why they deleted it!

Forgiveness, or even kindness, is not everyone's default! If anything, very few people have that kind of default in life, let alone in trauma and loss.

The next day was something I've never experienced or even known was possible. I woke with a non-consensual rage in me that desired to do harm. Growing up with abuse and neglect, I am all too familiar with anger. But this was not anger. This made anger pale in comparison. I no longer desired to make sure this child was safe. A monster resided in me that was all-consuming. I wanted to run them over with my car and make their mother watch as I ended their life. The experience was completely involuntary and nonconsensual on my part, but all the same, my entire existence became consumed with a desire to inflict harm.

This is NOT me! Not in any version of my trauma and my abuse-filled life had I ever desired for there to be harm to any of my afflicters. And believe me, they deserved it. Yet in this moment, I wanted to be the one to cause the suffering, not just for it to occur. I wanted the parents to hurt like I did!

I sat in this engulfing rage for 3 days, unable to eat, sleep or think about anything but my anger and desire for revenge. When I reflect honestly, I believe that rage was an easier emotion than the overwhelming sadness associated with my grief. The whole experience of her death and the reality of it seemed inconceivable, and the thought of processing or accepting myself as a potential murderer seemed easier to accept than the fact that my baby died... so horrifically and traumatically. That I would never hold her again! She didn't just pass away—she was deeply harmed by the actions of others, to the point where she believed the only way to escape the pain was to end her life.

I have always tried to teach my children that it's important for us to acknowledge and validate our emotions and allow them to be, but that it then becomes a choice whether or not we stay in that place. And that is the difference between being a victim or not.

It's not always easy to take your own advice. BUT I knew that I had to make a choice. I knew that if I stayed in this place of anger and rage, I would cook myself from the inside (I could feel it happening) and likely brew an aggressive cancer that would kill within a month. The experience of this rage is beyond my capabilities to adequately define with words. I was like a lobster in a pot that had been turned to full boil. The fight within me to NOT inflict harm, combined with the overwhelming desire to, was literally cooking me. I was dying. Even faster than I knew was possible.

So I had to let go. I had to choose life. I had to choose myself. And my girls.

Because anything else was the equivalent of drinking poison, hoping someone else is affected by it. The way I see it, the people who hurt Rylee—including the bully and the groomer—fall into one of two categories.

The first is someone trapped in a prison of guilt and remorse. A prison only they can free themselves from—by choosing to grow from this tragedy, to do better, to be better. And in doing so, honour Rylee's life in a meaningful way.

There is no version of me that desires for either of them (or anyone for that matter) to be stuck in guilt or remorse.

They are heavy and destructive emotions that rob your life of meaning, joy and purpose.

The second kind is more dangerous—narcissistic, perhaps sociopathic—someone who feels no real accountability and may go on to harm others.

But ultimately, neither of these scenarios are within my control and choosing to hold on to anger, rage or a desire for revenge only robs me of the opportunity to live (fully) in the present and robs my living children of not just their sister but also their mum. You can't do both. You cannot be in the present and future oriented, invested in learning to live and grieve simultaneously in a way facilitates living a joy-filled and rewarding life, but also consumed by anger, rage and/or invested in revenge. The second of which will neither bring her back nor appease the never-ending pain of her absence.

So let me tell you again. Hate is one of the most *expensive* emotions. Peace and joy can absolutely coexist with grief and loss.

But anger is the antithesis of peace.

It's not about denying anger at the injustices that contribute to our grief. It's about understanding that feeding and watering thoughts of anger or a desire for revenge is like wanting roses to grow, but fertilising the weeds that strangle and suffocate the roses.

I am not saying don't act. Perhaps someone has done something that needs to be addressed or penalised using the justice system. I'm just saying that with the very limited energy I had to survive the trauma and loss of my child, I had to make a very important decision about where that energy was best invested. And for me, it was in letting go... and choosing life.

Choosing forgiveness at the time wasn't about excusing or allowing the behaviours that contributed to Rylee's death. It was about freeing myself from the prison of anger–an anger that, if left unchecked, would've only harmed me.

I'm proud of myself for recognising that early on–for choosing life, love, and kindness over bitterness and revenge. It took courage, and I'm grateful I had it.

Resilience

I said yes to grief

I said yes to grief.

It wasn't graceful.

It wasn't poetic.

It was desperate, messy, and raw.

It was a whisper yes. Not because I wanted grief, but because I knew denying it would cost me everything else: my health, my sanity, my daughters, my soul. The weight of pretending I was 'strong' enough to overcome it would've crushed me.

So I surrendered.

Not in weakness, but in defiance of a culture that tells us the only options are to be consumed and destroyed by it or to move on quickly, to smile through the wreckage, to pretend we're okay.

I wasn't okay.

And I needed to not be okay–openly, unapologetically, fully.
Because my daughter had died.
Because the world I knew had shattered.
Because pretending it hadn't would have made a liar of my love for her.

So I leaned into grief.
Let it teach me.
Let it strip away every illusion I had about control, safety, fairness, or certainty.
I let it hurt. I let it howl. I let it hollow me out.
And somewhere in the hollowing, something unexpected happened.
I started to feel other things.
Not instead of grief.
But alongside it.

Moments of beauty.
A deep breath that felt sacred.
The feel of the sun warming my skin.
A laugh that surprised me.

The tenderness in the way Zali or Mia looked at me when they thought I wasn't watching.
At first, I felt guilt.
How dare I laugh?
How dare I feel anything other than heartbreak?
But I came to understand something profound:
Grief and joy are not rivals.
They are twins born of the same love.
You do not betray your sorrow by welcoming joy.
You do not erase your joy by honouring your sorrow.
They can, and do, exist in the same space.
I learned to live in the *and*...

Grieve *and* breathe.
Cry *and* laugh.
Ache *and* dance.
Remember Rylee *and* make new memories.

This is what no one prepares you for:
The paradox of grief is that it doesn't shrink your life—it stretches it. It breaks you open in a way that, if you let it, makes room for more.
More feeling.
More truth.
More reverence.
More gratitude for the smallest, quietest, most ordinary miracles.

Saying yes to grief taught me to stop trying to get back to *who I was before*. That version of me is gone. But who I am now is wiser, softer and stronger in the most unexpected ways. Because I chose to live fully–not in spite of the grief, but with it. I let grief take up space at the table, but I didn't let it sit alone.

> I made room for joy.
> For peace.
> For meaning.
> And I discovered they could all cohabitate in the same soul. Grief is a visitor that never truly leaves–but it no longer controls the house.
> It sits beside love.
> It rests next to gratitude.
> And every now and then, they look at one another and nod–understanding that their presence doesn't cancel the other's out, but affirms it.
>
> That is the truth no one tells you:
> Grief is the cost of love.
> But gratitude...
> *Gratitude* is what reminds you that the love was–and still is–real. And that is what makes it all worth surviving.

In reflecting on what has played the biggest part in my learning to live and grieve simultaneously, I realise that in the early days and every day since... ***I said YES to grief.***

That's not to say it was easy, or even that I was consciously aware that I was doing it. And obviously, initially, we all struggled with denial. After all, it was unforeseen and so incomprehensible. But denial is the brain's initial way of coping with something that seems too overwhelming to comprehend. It's a protective mechanism because the trauma of your reality is too much for the human psyche to bare and so in its wisdom, the brain has the ability to cushion you, in part, from the severity of this newfound reality. As amazing as that is, denial doesn't serve you moving forward. It does the opposite. Denial prevents you from opening up to the possibilities and beauty that life and even death have to offer.

A lot of the (previous) trauma in my life was not met with denial but rather an element of radical acceptance that said, 'Okay, what am I going to do about or in response to this?' I never wanted to be anyone's victim. And I most certainly wasn't going to let the traumatic life events of my childhood and youth define my future or determine where I was heading in life. I think that this ability to step out from under the sometimes instinctual response of denial and move, albeit at times slowly, toward radical acceptance in life, is what opens us up to more living.

Please note that I write now from a place of reflection and am by no means implying that things felt simple or clearcut as they unfolded, but rather that I now benefit from the clarity of hindsight. Grief is an absolute bitch. And I spent so much of the first year and a half unsure I would even survive. Not because I thought I would harm myself, but rather because the depth of the harm inflicted by the trauma of her death and subsequent loss felt as though it was not something I could survive and therefore was speeding up my untimely demise - what it feels like to be dying of a broken heart.

Rylee passed on a Thursday night. From that night we were surrounded by family holding space for us in any way they could which was mostly just bouts of silent presence and intermittent walks to the beach, between the exhaustion induced naps from which I would wake so nauseated (and vomiting) from the realisation that it hadn't in fact been a nightmare at all, but instead was a living nightmare from which there was no escape.

I would find myself crouched in the doorway to the bathroom, white knuckle gripping the door frame, screaming the same horrific sound that involuntarily left my body that night once confronted with her lifeless body. I remember saying to my brother-in-law on the Saturday, things like... 'We aren't having a funeral! You aren't supposed to have a fucking funeral for your child!' and 'I can't be the one to call and organise the cremation, I just can't!' Whilst he was so lovingly willing to take on any burden I deemed too heavy, it didn't take me long to move from that denial to a more open-hearted place where I attempted to replace denial with acceptance.

I didn't know that was what I was doing at the time. I just remember that sitting in denial made the pain feel so much worse. Denial was sickening, but necessary. Denial would allow a momentary reprieve from the agony of the realisation of her passing. But it was only momentary, and the longer you tried to stay in that place of denial, the less anything at all made sense and the more it hurt.

Don't get me wrong, there was no making sense out of her suicide. There was only what would turn out to be radical acceptance. Had I stayed in this place of denial, who knows how different and stunted our grief would've been. (I'm not saying people should do things that they absolutely cannot, and am an advocate for asserting the boundaries necessary to protect your sanity.) But for me, these things were said from a place of denying her death as a reality rather than asserting any boundaries. Like somehow, if we didn't have a funeral or I didn't have to be confronted by the conversation involving calling to organise a cremation for my own child... that somehow the fact that she was deceased and would never be mine to hold again or speak to, would not be a fact at all.

My brain was scrambling, desperately trying to not only make sense out of the incomprehensible but return to some kind of familiar, in an attempt to protect my sanity. But as I sat with my grief and felt the love-induced heaviness of it, I realised that funerals aren't just about us. They aren't actually about us at all. They are about the person who is gone and are intended as an opportunity for any and all who loved, cared for and were impacted by that person to acknowledge their life and farewell them. They are an attempt at some kind of closure that, particularly in this instance, was important for so many more than just us.

As much as I believe people would've understood if we had said we just couldn't do it, I think we would have regretted it massively had we not. Not just for ourselves but for her friends, peers and teachers who also lost Rylee. The loss and its associated grief wasn't just ours. Rylee was such a beautiful soul, whose life touched and positively impacted so many, and I realised whilst we were right to not want a funeral, we were also right in acknowledging the wider need to celebrate (and acknowledge) Rylee's life.

It's a powerful and valuable part of everyone's grief, particularly when there is no warning and will be no other form of closure. There was also the fact that a lot of children (teens) needed their grief and loss acknowledged, and having a celebration of life facilitated that. I can only imagine how much more their hearts would hurt had there been no farewell.

Looking back, I realise that this was the first of many times I said yes to grief. I'm not sure whether it was the Sunday or the Monday, but I had moved out from under the heaviness of denial just enough to be able to say, 'It's okay, I will call to arrange the cremation.' By this stage, I felt it needed to be me. She was, after all, my baby. The man on the end of the line delivered each question with such empathy and compassion and facilitated a comfortable, if not peace-giving, conversation around my daughter's death. He was so respectful as he collected the information he needed.

I was so scared to make that call.

To this day, I appreciate how he referred to Rylee as Rylee and not 'your daughter', 'her body' or 'the deceased'. He explained everything that would happen, saying that they would let me know once Rylee was with them, which he later did. He definitely made what could've been an added trauma a seamless, respectful and compassionate experience.

Without realising it, he was my death doula.

The cremation facility was quite a distance from us and I was worried about whether or not her ashes would be ready for pick up prior to, or in time for, the Celebration of Life the following weekend. I was having part of her ashes put into a mini heart-shaped urn for her older brother to take with him back to Melbourne, and was worried it wouldn't be done in time. This gentleman not only made sure everything was seamless and happened in time, he even brought her ashes to the Gold Coast for me to pick up with greater ease.

When he was organising this with me, he said, 'I will bring Rylee with me after work and meet you.' The power and impact of this man's emotional intelligence, empathy and compassion in referring to her as Rylee instead of 'ashes', particularly during a time likely to still be seeped in shock and denial following the loss of one's child, is something I will forever be grateful for.

The point of these examples is to acknowledge that had I not been able to say yes to grief, just enough to move from complete denial to attempting acceptance, I would not have been open to planning a celebration of life, and I would've had someone else plan her cremation. Both things I now know I would have later regretted massively. Whilst most of her celebration of life is a blur, the planning of it isn't. The beauty and connection facilitated by it aren't either. The ability for her friends and teachers to gather under an incredibly beautiful big old tree on the school grounds (later lovingly referred to by many as Rylee's tree and where you will often still see flowers left) didn't just facilitate an acknowledgement of her life and a farewell, but also provided somewhere those that loved her could go if they wanted to feel close to her. As she was being cremated and there would be no tombstone/grave site, this ended up being of more value to more people than we would first anticipate.

I cannot tell you how much it would mean to me when so many times I would be struggling emotionally, only to do school pick up (or attend the markets at the school grounds on a weekend) and see the flowers someone had left on her tree. I was speaking to a teacher whose office was right by the big tree, not that long after she passed, when they told me how beautiful a reminder it had become of having Rylee in their life and how grateful they were that on their more difficult days, they could just look outside and feel connected to her. All this beauty came about as a result of having the courage to step (to begin with, albeit momentarily) out from under the heaviness of denial and begin to say yes to grief!

As I continue to learn how to live and grieve simultaneously, I allow the sadness. I speak honestly and vulnerably about both (life and grief) as and when I need to. I acknowledge the presence of her absence and protect myself and my children with boundaries at times that feel overwhelming, like anniversaries, but I also make sure I don't self-isolate and unnecessarily withdraw.

There is a difference in protecting your peace/energy when you have little to nothing to give or need time and space to process, and pulling away from people. They say it takes a village to raise a child. It definitely takes a village to survive the loss of one.

Whilst I have never felt so broken and so much deeply unsettling pain, I have also never felt so seen, valued and loved. The people that banded around us in those early days, that contributed to the gofundme that ultimately probably saved my life, that brought food, meals, flowers, cards... the thoughts, messages and silent prayers for our broken hearts and aching souls became a sea of love that washed over us and the effects of which continue to positively impact all of us to this day. People who didn't even know us even contributed... the village, made up of so many and something I didn't know I needed!

I heard once that when dolphins birth in the wild the other dolphins will form a kind of circle around the birthing mother in order to protect her from harm and allow her to labour and birth instinctively and that once the baby dolphin emerges the other dolphins nudge it to the surface for its first breath allowing the birthing mother time to deal the overwhelm of what's just happened to her. I don't know if this is true, but the village of people that came together after her death to support us felt a lot like that circle and although it was a death not a birth people held space for me, for my overwhelm and for my children in a way that protected us from the further harm of worrying about bills and how to feed ourselves in those early days and contributed to us being able to eventually find our footing on what has most definitely proved to be a lot more stable ground than what would've been without their love, empathy and support. I will be forever grateful!

I'm so proud of each of us for how we have handled the last few years and who we have each become. I'm proud of myself and grateful that, as uncomfortable as it was that I was able to lean into grief and get to know it rather than deny it. I see beauty in every day... in me... in my children and my relationships. I love being alive (as uncomfortable a journey grief continues to be at times) and understand that grief is the manifestation of all the unexpressed love we didn't get to share with the person we lost, and am able to, for the better part, reframe it as that. Which is A LOT nicer to live with than anger or hate.

Resilience through gratitude

Since losing Rylee and especially in those early months to a year, when people would hear me tell the story of or details about her death or any part of what we had been through, their response was almost always the same–right down to the wording: *'How are you surviving this? I couldn't... I wouldn't! There is no way I would survive!'*

You hear these same words enough, and it starts to make you question. What am I doing that would make (almost) EVERYONE ask this same question? Convinced that whatever it was I was doing was somehow superhuman and not something they would be capable of.

It wasn't until I hit a momentary experience of *poor me/ why me* that I realised what it was that had become my armour for initially surviving, but then also learning how to not just survive, but thrive, in this kind of trauma and loss.

As mentioned earlier, Rylee jumped off my balcony 33 stories high with myself and her sisters home and I had to go down and find her. The girls who were aged 11 years and 13 years at the time heard my screams from 33 stories up, so they came down (and saw her body on the ground surrounded by broken glass) before being separated from me immediately by well-intentioned police officers trying to shield them from further trauma. I mention this so that you understand how and why people had been saying what they were saying in response to hearing about her death. The trauma of it caused what I would equate to being a traumatic brain injury for me. My brain (and soul) were so significantly injured that night that years later, I still have issues with remembering things prior to her death. I am unsure if this injury will be lifelong or if, in time, my brain will heal and my memory will improve. But in the meantime, I simply apologise and explain to people (when necessary) that my daughter passed away and that the trauma of the experience has affected my memory.

Anyway, back to my *why me* moment and the realisation that accompanied it.

I remember feeling angry that life had been so fucking unkind to me since I was little. Why did I have to go through so much pain, abuse, neglect? Why couldn't I just be loved? When would I ever catch a break?

I felt like I had spent my entire life bracing for impact or getting back up from the last assault, insult or injury. I really thought now that I was in my 40's surely life was going to start being a bit kinder to me!

Prior to losing Rylee, people who would hear about my life would often be gobsmacked, saying things like, *How are you this person after all of that? How are you so kind and together? How have you done so well for yourself after having all of this thrown at you?*

I would shrug it off not giving it much thought. Until this day that is. My *why me* downward spiral of WTAF is going on?

It was during this momentary downward spiral that I realised that if it wasn't for everything I had been through, I don't think I would've survived either. Whilst I wouldn't wish any of it on anyone, having lived through what I had, saw a resilience borne of gratitude develop from an early age that strengthened with time, practice and no shortage of life challenges to apply it to.

The thing is, I had been doing it so long I didn't even realise it was my default or something that had so intrinsically become a part of my everyday lived experience. You see, when we were little (because of abuse and neglect), if you were kind to me, I was so grateful; if you fed me, I was so grateful. I wasn't expectant, which made being extremely grateful so easy. Any act of kindness was almost overwhelming; seen as an act of unconditional love and appreciated so much that it helped stain my soul with the knowing that there were in fact, kind people in the world. It gave me hope and helped me realise that I did not need to be the sum of my origins. That where I came from did not need to (and would not) determine how far or where I was going in life.

You really do never know just how much a simple act of kindness can mean to someone's life journey!

My brain learnt to look for the positives, for the things to be grateful for. Turns out they are VERY easy to find, and there is ALWAYS something to be grateful for. And when you start doing it daily, it becomes second nature.

I remember when we were planning the celebration of life, and the lady was asking about Rylee. I explained that had I known she was only on loan to me for 15 years, I wouldn't have done anything differently. I loved her with every fibre of my being, and she knew that. I was so grateful to have been her mum.

Fast forward a couple of weeks, and a friend took me to a bathhouse to soak amongst the trees so we could talk, cry and as it turned out, laugh together. It was the first time I had laughed since she passed. I was overcome by the weirdest combination of humour, connection, sadness and guilt for laughing or finding joy in something. Laughter wasn't familiar anymore and felt like something that would no longer be allowed to reside in the same space as where grief and trauma now lived.

I told her the details of Rylee's death, how the glass ceiling of the turning circle of my building had broken her fall and how, because of that she looked so peaceful, as though she was just lying there, face down with her hands up around her head. Even the police later said they didn't know how this was possible. I explained that I was so grateful for this and that her body wasn't broken apart by the fall or the impact, as I think I would've looked for the next truck and run in front of it had that been the case. I was grateful that what the girls saw was contained and appeared peaceful rather than inciting more trauma.

I will never forget how this friend looked at me, so puzzled and with tears in her eyes and said, 'Es, my god, if you are talking about things you are grateful for after what you've just been through, I think you're going to be okay!'

She couldn't have been more right!

Use gratitude like an insurance policy

Gratitude became my default–long before I realised it would be my greatest resource in learning how to live and grieve simultaneously. And to be clear, I'm not talking about bypassing pain or denying the trauma of loss. This isn't about waiting for life to fall apart and then slapping gratitude on top like a Band-Aid either. Yes, it can help in those moments—but what I'm really talking about is the power of gratitude when practiced daily. One that becomes so natural, so deeply woven into your being, that it becomes a subconscious lifeline. A kind of emotional insurance policy, if you like.

If we're alive and loving anyone or anything, we're always at risk of significant loss. But when gratitude is your default, it shifts everything. It doesn't cancel the grief, but it helps you hold it. It doesn't erase the heartbreak, but it softens the sharp edges. Gratitude is what makes it possible to live and grieve simultaneously—to keep loving life, even in the face of loss. And in some ways, because of it.

I like to think of gratitude the way we think about car insurance. If you own a car, you insure it. You may resent the payments, but you accept them as necessary. Why? Because you understand the risk of ownership. Even if the car never leaves your driveway, it can still be damaged by hail, theft, or even a passing vehicle. You don't have to be reckless to experience loss; just owning something valuable makes you vulnerable. If you are fortunate, you will pay the premium across the lifespan without ever needing to make a claim. And in the event that you do need to make a claim, doing so doesn't remove the after effects or consequences, but it does make sure they don't ruin you. We don't insure our assets expecting to make a claim; we do it because we know the cost of not being prepared could be far greater.

Now consider life.

If we are alive, if we love, we are always at risk of loss. It's not if storms come—it's when. Gratitude is like the emotional insurance policy for our lives. It doesn't prevent hardship or protect us from pain. But it softens the blow, grounds us in what remains, and helps us recover when life crack us open in a way that might otherwise destroy us.

Just like insurance, you may not fully appreciate its value until you need it most. But building a gratitude practice now ensures that when life hits hard, you won't be completely unprotected.

Maybe you're in the thick of grief right now—and gratitude doesn't feel like a familiar practice in your life. If that's you, please stay with me. I'll come back to why starting a gratitude practice now, even in the midst of pain, can gently begin to shift things.

But if, by some grace, you've found this book before life comes for you - before the bottom falls out—then I urge you: listen closely. Because (as I keep saying) the truth is, if you're alive, breathing, and especially if you're loving anything or anyone, you are always living at risk of significant loss.

Anything that can happen can happen at any time. Now—I don't say that to scare you. This isn't about living in fear or spiralling into anxiety. Instead, I invite you to acknowledge that truth in a way that empowers you. Because life is short. Tomorrow is never promised. So why not live now—fully, consciously, and with presence?

Nothing supports that kind of presence quite like gratitude. Not surface-level thankfulness, but an embodied, daily practice of noticing what still is—even while we hold what's been lost, or what could be. Gratitude anchors us. It softens our grip on the wheel of life, the part of us that thinks we need control and opens our eyes to what matters most—right here, in this moment.

How to make friends with gratitude in the thick of grief

When you're in the depths of grief, gratitude might feel impossible—maybe even offensive. You're not expected to feel thankful for what happened. This isn't about finding silver linings in your pain or coating it in toxic positivity. It's about finding small anchors to help you survive it.

Here's how to begin, gently:

1. Start small–painfully small

Look for one thing a day that doesn't hurt. Not something huge. Not a big 'win'. Maybe it's:

- The warmth of your tea
- A moment of quiet
- A friend who texted back
- A bird you heard this morning
- The fact that you got out of bed

Write it down. Or whisper it. Or... just think it. That's enough.

2. Call it what it is

It's okay to say, 'I don't feel grateful, but I'm trying to notice what still matters.'

That counts.

That is gratitude.

No pretending required.

3. Allow the duality of gratitude and grief

Gratitude doesn't cancel grief. They can sit side by side.

You can say:

- 'I miss them so much, and I'm grateful I had them.'
- 'I'm hurting today, and I'm thankful for the quiet.'

This is where the shift begins: not in replacing your pain, but in widening your capacity to hold both love and loss in the same parts of your heart and soul.

4. Use a simple prompt

Each day, try finishing these sentences:

- 'Today, I'm grateful for... '
- '... helped me feel more human.'
- 'Even though today was hard I... '

5. Trust the slow magic

Over time, these small acknowledgments rewire your inner world. They don't fix grief, but they do help you stay soft, awake, and connected to life, even in your sadness and pain.

> *Remember–gratitude is not a betrayal of your grief. It's a companion that helps you survive it.*

The daily practice we didn't know would be our life raft

Whenever the kids would return from being away from us, whether at a sleepover, day out, or even just returning from their day at school, we would often ask, 'What was the best part of your day?'

Sometimes they would answer quickly and enthusiastically, other times you'd see them pondering their options and looking for the 'winner'. Regardless, there was always an answer. Then we would ask, 'What was the worst part of your day?' Again, the answer may come easily and quickly to mind, other times (and to be honest) more often than not, they would respond with 'There wasn't one!'

If they did respond with something that was the worst part, it would allow us to explore their response. Say the answer was 'The school canteen ran out of the drink I wanted', it would allow us to encourage the reflection that if that's the worst part of your day, that's a pretty good day. To which they would smile and agree. If the response was 'such and such was unkind or a bully', we would help them explore the person's actions, reflect to see if somehow they contributed to the situation and in most cases reframe it and help them understand that someone else's actions or behaviours are very rarely about you.

For the better part, as they grew, I noticed that most of the time their response to 'what was the worst part of their day or experience away' was met with 'Nothing, it was all great!' The thing about priming the brain to initially look for the best of something is that it starts collating examples and collecting evidence in an attempt to respond. And because there is no shortage of things to feel good about or grateful for, they end up with a whole pile of stuff from which they have to pick the best. Then, when you ask the brain to tell you what was the worst, it's still fresh with so much positive evidence that backs feelings of joy and gratitude that I'm not surprised they would respond as they did... 'Nothing, it was all good!'

It also helps me realise that when they do have something as 'the worst', it's worth visiting and unpacking with them to see if it really was negative and if so, how it impacted them and what they might do differently next time or if it just wasn't quite as awesome as the rest of their experiences. Without realising it, I had spent years priming my children's brains for a resilience borne of gratitude that did not need to be facilitated by the same traumas and abuse that mine had.

Fun Fact: It's impossible to feel shitty and grateful at the same time. If you don't agree, give it a try ;-)

If you want to weave your way out of a negative headspace, gratitude is usually one of the quickest and most effective ways to do so. Not to mention, once you grab the string of gratitude, you will not find the end. There is never an end to that which we can be grateful for!

An example of this is when we might find ourselves irritated at someone close to us for something they didn't do, but if we start thinking about all the things about them that we are grateful for, and the things they do do, the list grows immediately and far outweighs the negative we might've previously been focusing on. Our brain also responds by releasing the hormones and chemical messengers that facilitate us feeling the way we are thinking. We suddenly feel overwhelmed with love for them, which is a much better and nicer place to communicate frustration from (if the frustration is actually worth communicating now we've had time to process and didn't act or respond from anger).

Inversely, if I spend time thinking about and watering (if you like) thoughts of sadness or anger, my brain will then cooperate by releasing hormones and chemicals that facilitate me feeling the way I am thinking.

You see, we aren't responsible for every thought that pops into our heads, but we are responsible for what we do with them. And practicing gratitude daily most certainly facilitates a more present, joyful and rewarding life experience.

For those currently in the thick of grief, trauma and its associated sense of overwhelming loss who may not have previously given much thought or practice to gratitude, I have great news! Without sounding condescending ...it's never too late to start.

There are always things to be grateful for; we just need to look for them. The powerful impact gratitude has on what is currently likely to look and feel overwhelmingly sad or even anger-inducing is beyond what you might imagine is possible right now. Sadness, anger, denial and all of our negative emotions we so easily associate with grief are usually familiar and may even feel safe because of that familiarity. Maybe even easy. Til now, you've probably had quite an intimate relationship with perhaps all of them. And there is nothing wrong with that. I just want you to know life can be better than that. Better than settling for safe and familiar sadness or anger.

I can totally relate to the feeling that *this just must be me now? Forever broken and feeling like an alien on this planet, dying a slow death of a broken heart.* I felt like no one could or would ever possibly understand the overwhelming depths of my sadness or just how absolutely shattered my poor heart was and (I thought) forever will be. Even now, as I wrote those last couple of sentences, my eyes involuntarily leak tears of empathy for that prior version of myself who couldn't see the forest for the trees.

But the tears are temporary and replaced with pride like that of a parent who has watched their baby learn to walk or ride a bike. I am so proud that I didn't give up on myself.

That I was able to use gratitude like an incredibly powerful glue that helps hold the seams together of the Me I became in the aftermath of my trauma.

I didn't put myself back together.

I couldn't, because that version of me no longer existed, and I think that is what scares us the most in the initial aftermath of significant loss. The perceived loss of identity. The loss of self as we know it. Gratitude is like the medicine for the soul though, and something that is available to all of us, all of the time.

You don't come out of trauma and loss the same person you went in. Positively or negatively... it changes you. That change is a choice and one that most of us make subconsciously. If you are not proud of the version of you that you have or are becoming in the aftermath of your trauma, loss and/or grief, then I would encourage you to consider making conscious choices about the things you do and can control moving forward. You may currently be acting and reacting from subconscious, outdated ways of relating that could stem all the way back to your childhood. Either way, if the outcome is negative and not lending itself to creating the kind of life you desire and deserve, then it is definitely time to change something.

Gratitude is NOT the same as toxic positivity

Whilst I do advocate for and am 100 % living proof of the power of daily practice of gratitude and impacting your life in the positive ways I've mentioned, I'm by no means talking about toxic positivity.

I am not talking about just lacing everything with a positive outlook and denying, dismissing or suppressing the presence or validity of negative emotions like sadness, anger or frustration. **I'm not!**

I am absolutely advocating for you to feel those emotions. I am a hundred percent advocating for you to acknowledge every emotion as it arises, sit with it, allow it to be validated (if it's valid) and definitely allow it to be.

But I'm also advocating for the fact that once we've done all of that, it then becomes a choice whether or not we stay in that place. And that's the difference between being a victim or not.

That's a very confronting thing for some people to hear because we don't often think of ourselves as taking on the victim role or playing the victim. But if we are able to experience our emotions and validate them, but then we just stay and sit in that place, we're choosing that. We're choosing that negative emotion. We're choosing to continue that experience. It IS actually a choice whether or not we stay in that place.

Gratitude opens the door that facilitates the acknowledgement that whilst I did not or may not choose the environmental factors of what's happening in and around my life, I do get to control the things that I can. And what I can control is the way that I perceive what happens in and around my life and I get to choose my response. Am I going to get stuck drinking the poison, hoping someone else dies, or am I going to choose life? Am I going to acknowledge my negative emotions, allow them to be, sit with them but then take accoutability and actually choose what I do with that thought.

For instance, I recently had what should have been my daughter's 18th birthday. And obviously, there was no shortage of thoughts, just uninvited coming into my mind about the negatives of it. All the things that I will have to live without in her absence and throughout my grief journey. All the things that I'll have to navigate that should have been things that I would share with her. So all these uninvited and negative thoughts pop in.

And whilst I don't choose those thoughts, I do get to choose what I do with them. If I sit and feed and water negative thoughts, thoughts of sadness, if I then play sad songs on repeat, my body is going to respond by releasing hormones that make me feel the way I'm thinking.

Whilst the sadness associated with these thoughts appears valid, this is the point at which we give our power away. If I stay there and I feed and water and feel justified in my sadness, anger or any other negative emotion, I'm actually growing that by what I'm doing with the feeding and watering. I'm now going to facilitate a hormonal response to the thoughts that I've fed and watered that then makes me feel the way I am thinking. Now I can feel it. Now my heart's racing or the tears are coming, my stomach is in knots and there is a painful lump in my throat. I can feel it throughout my body. I'm having this physical experience of the emotions in response to the thoughts that I have sat with too long and fed and watered.

It is NOT *the chicken or the egg* shit. Which one came first?! The thought came first. We do something with it. Our body responds with the hormones that create the 'feelings' or emotions, and we usually react or respond from that emotionally charged place. I didn't feel sad, and so then started thinking sad thoughts!

Don't get me wrong. I'm in the thick of grief. Sometimes sadness needs to be sat with. Sometimes it's back as a visitor that needs you to just hold its hand, and allow it to be. But if in holding its hand, I'm then not getting out of bed, playing sad songs, or I'm dwelling on all the things that I think that I will miss out on… I've passively allowed the thoughts of sadness to stay too long and, in doing so, released the hormones that facilitate my body feeling sorrow. I'm now feeling depressed. That hormonal release then facilitates an ease with which I do more of what I've been doing, feeling sorry for myself and not getting out of bed, not making it to the gym, cutting people off, self-isolating. You can see how it can be a spiral.

Be mindful of how long you dwell on negative emotions.

Again, I want to validate that you are not responsible for the first thought that pops into your mind, but you are responsible for what you do with it from there. So if we find that we are experiencing life in a way that doesn't serve us, the good news is we can reverse engineer that to reveal the kind of lived experience we desire. We can take a step back and see that if I got to choose how I wanted to feel in my body, how I wanted to perceive my life… and this isn't what I would choose, then let's reverse engineer how I got here because it's pretty easy to do once we start breaking it down backwards.

If I understand that I didn't choose the thought but that I did do something with it that then created a release of hormones and now I'm feeling the way I was thinking, we start to realise that if I want to feel differently I do so by beginning to acknowledge that I can change the way that I think about and view my lived experience.

And that's the thing that I can control! My mindset is the story that I tell myself when no one else is listening.

It's how I view my life and everything that unfolds in and around it. It's how personally I take the behaviours of others and how much I let that affect my physiology, and then my internal lived experience. And that my internal lived experience of how I feel hormonally then starts to impact my external experience of life, because if I allow myself to be overcome by sadness and hormones that feed a feeling of depression, then I'm more likely to make choices like self-isolating or staying in bed. So now my external lived experience is being negatively impacted.

Some people will say, 'But that's just me or him. That's him. That's how he's always been. He can't change it.' Or 'I can't change it. You don't understand. I've always been like that.' I'm here to tell you the good news is you can (change)! We all have the capacity to change. The confines of this book don't allow me to delve too deep into neuroplasticity, but I would encourage you, if you don't know what it is, to go and do some research because we all have the capacity to actually rewire our brains.

The beautiful thing about this is that even if the daily or regular practice of gratitude is not something you are familiar with, it is something that you can start today and use to rewire your brain in a way that sees it become a new and very powerful subconscious resource and default setting.

It is important to acknowledge that the ability to do so does not necessitate trauma as a precursor. You don't need to have had a shitty life to date or significant trauma like I mentioned occurred in my childhood, in order to establish a resilience borne of gratitude! (I hope for your sake that you haven't!).

The beautiful thing about gratitude is that it's available to all of us, at all times and there is ALWAYS something to be grateful for!

Life is happening for me, not to me

If your endeavour is to experience a rewarding life in spite of any challenges, traumas or losses along the way, then you will need to check which lens through which you habitually view your life. The shift to viewing life as happening for me, not to me, is one that will yield rewards of which the evidence is simply waiting for you to take notice. In order to think that life is happening to you, you have to take on the victim role. You're a victim of what's happening, and although this may not have occurred on a conscious level, it will rob you of joy, contentment and satisfaction all the same.

My life is amazing. Every day I experience amazing health and get to still be here and love this life... It's a hundred percent happening for me.

Remember, our brains find what they look for. A good analogy for this is when you decide to buy a Mercedes, you'll start seeing them everywhere. It's because our energy goes where our focus is. It's also why when you see someone across the shop (that you don't know), but if you stare at them, they'll turn and look directly at you. We have such a powerful force that is our energy, and where we put our energy pulls more of that into our life.

So, if you have a pessimistic tendency to view everything in life as shitty, your brain will go on a fact-finding mission to collate evidence to support that viewpoint and reinforce it. Your brain will respond with 'You're right!... Look at this shitty weather... shitty people... shitty job... shitty car!' Whatever it is, you will find a way to validate your lived experience based on what you're looking for.

And similarly, if you're an optimist who is looking for the positive, your brain will find no shortage of ways to validate that lived experience. And I'm not talking about toxic optimism that implies that everything happens for a reason in an attempt to make the whole lived experience a positive one. Some parts of life suck! You don't have to find a way to describe it that laces it in optimism and says that this has to be a good experience. And that's by no means what I'm trying to do. I'm saying that in spite of the fact that challenges will present themselves throughout your life (that suck), you get to choose how you respond to those things and control the fact that you can actually continue to move forward with your life, in spite of your suffering.

Perception is like heads or tails—but YOU get to choose

No matter how devastating, heartbreaking, or soul-crushing the storm in your life may be, you don't have to stay stuck in it. It doesn't have to be the end of you. It might be the end of life as you knew it. It might change who you are, how you see the world and what you value. But it is not the end of you.

What comes next is shaped by your willingness to engage consciously with your life—not just letting it happen to you like a series of assaults, but choosing to show up and navigate even the most painful moments with presence, self-compassion, and intention. It is possible to move through loss, trauma, and adversity in a way that still allows your soul to be nourished, your heart to be fulfilled, and your life to hold meaning. But that possibility hinges on one thing: How you see yourself in relationship to your life and its unfolding.

You came here to live. *To really live.*

You get one red-hot crack at this life—I promise it's happening for you, not just to you. How you experience it, especially in the face of hardship, comes down to your mindset and your choice to stay in the driver's seat.

> *The driver isn't responsible for the condition of the road or the scenery along the way. What the driver is responsible for is how they respond—how they steer, brake, and adjust when the road changes.*

Picture yourself driving through a hilly landscape. You don't always know what's ahead–around the bend, beyond the next rise. Sometimes, the view takes your breath away: golden sunsets, wide-open skies, beauty you couldn't have planned. Other times, you hit a patch of ice and spin, nearly losing control. The shock of that moment–the near miss–might leave you shaken, even fearful.

Now comes the choice:

Do you let fear take over, park the car, and insist it's too dangerous to keep driving? Maybe you even get out and decide to walk, convincing yourself that it's safer on foot–though you have no idea what dangers might lie ahead that way either.

Or, do you stay in the driver's seat? Do you move forward with greater care around blind corners, while still allowing yourself to witness the beauty, trust the journey, and adjust as needed? You're still in control of how and when you move. That power remains yours.

The same applies to life. Our quality of life isn't determined by our ability to control everything around us–it's shaped by how we interpret the journey and respond to its twists and turns.

You may not have chosen the loss you're facing. Rarely do we. However, your ability to navigate it–especially if your perspective has been shaped by a mindset that seeks meaning or gratitude even in difficulty—makes a tangible difference. Because loss is a part of being human, and how your brain is wired before loss—whether to look for danger or for hope—will influence how you process and adapt after.

Now, let me be clear: having a *glass half full* mindset won't protect you from the pain of grief. But it will support your ability to integrate grief without being consumed by it.

Preparing ourselves for the inevitability of loss starts long before it arrives. It begins with how we meet life as it is—with all its unpredictability, expectations, detours, and gifts.

That being said, I understand that the early days of grief are not the ideal time to rebuild your entire worldview. The good news is, if you're here now—even in the thick of it—it's not too late to begin gently shifting your perspective. Not to erase the pain, but to give yourself a way to keep going. To stay in the driver's seat. To navigate forward, even if the road looks nothing like the one you imagined.

Our perception shapes how we interpret the world—what happens around us, what happens to us, and how we make meaning of it all. Most people go through life holding tightly to fixed interpretations of themselves, others, and their experiences. But in this rapidly changing world, we're being called to soften our grip—to become more flexible in how we see everything: our pain, our purpose, our relationships, our past, and even our potential.

The beauty is, perception is not fixed. Whether or not we recognise it in ourselves, we're constantly witnessing the human capacity for change—messy, uncomfortable, transformative change. How we choose to see our story, our suffering, our circumstances, and even our future—matters more than ever. And the good news? We can always choose to see differently.

The thing about perception is this - your viewpoint or interpretation of something is determined by where you are viewing it from. Say we were all sitting in a circle, looking at a small child sitting cross-legged on the floor. What you see may differ from what I see, depending on where in the circle we are sitting. I may see their face, whilst you might see the back of their head. Arguing over the view doesn't change mine or your interpretation. However, if either of us wants to view things differently, we simply need to get up out of our seat and reposition ourselves. Often in life, we assume a viewpoint or perception that doesn't or no longer serves us, and we need to view it differently. It's about having the courage to get uncomfortable and 'get up out of our seat' in life.

Another beneficial analogy is to think of your perception like that of a lens on a camera through which you see the world. Just like changing the lens alters how you see that which you are looking at, changing your perception of trauma, grief, loss, love, happiness, contentment, etc can completely alter your life experience in a way that doesn't demonise nor glorify the presence of any, but rather facilitates radical acceptance of all that is. And it's not the thing being viewed that changed. It's the way we are viewing it!

Welcome to a peace you didn't know was possible.

Understanding that, consciously or subconsciously, we choose our perception is the first step to empowering ourselves. We can start to become aware of our biases and begin taking conscious accountability for them.

Believe me, your energy is better spent on that which you can control.

We cannot and do not control other people. We do not have control over a lot of what will happen in our lives, and even to us. We can however, control how we interpret and react to what happens in our lives, around us and even to us.

It's like *heads or tails*–only you get to choose!

I cannot control or change the actions of others that harmed my daughter. I cannot control or change my daughter's actions that ended her life. I cannot control or change the fact that she is forever 15 and will never be mine to hold again. I cannot control every thought that pops into my mind, but I can control what I do with them. What I can control is who and where I choose to give the limited resource that is my energy to, and whether or not I give my power away. I can control how I view her presence in my life and what I perceive her purpose here to be. I can choose to cultivate gratitude and kindness, and decide how to move forward with my life.

Everything is a choice. We just make so many choices in our everyday lives on autopilot that we often forget that everything is actually a choice.

It's a choice to get out of bed. It's a choice to not get out of bed. You didn't 'not get out of bed' because you couldn't.

Getting dressed is a choice. Staying in your pyjamas is a choice. Speaking up and saying you are not okay is a choice. Staying quiet about not being ok is a choice. Saying yes to grief is a choice. Staying in denial is a choice. When you start using an addictive substance like alcohol or smoking it's a choice. When you are addicted it is still a choice it's just one made more difficult to stop because of the complex nature of addiction. Seeking help for addiction is a choice. Not seeking help is also a choice.

The thing about gratitude is that if you practice it enough, it becomes the default go-to setting of your brain that ends up feeling as involuntary as addiction. However, like addiction... You still always have a choice.

There were times in my grief where I would feel a lot like I imagine a smoker would when they look down and realise they've lit up yet another one, and they hadn't even (consciously) realised they had made the decision to. I would find myself saying how grateful I was about so much, so often, that I came to realise how difficult it is for me to have any lengthy or meaningful conversation without mentioning gratitude.

Although the practice may be new to you and seem like effort to start, I promise you your brain will reward the effort. If you do anything enough, you will train your brain to innately do or seek more of that. Not only will it become easier and more instinctive, but each time you do it your brain releases feel-good hormones that make depressive symptoms and sitting too long in sadness difficult to maintain.

Taming the ego

It's the ego that whispers, 'If only we had known, they'd still be here.' This instinctive response after losing someone to suicide often isn't grounded in truth—it's rooted in our desperate need to make sense of the senseless. But clinging to that thought only deepens our suffering. It keeps us stuck in guilt, regret or remorse, replaying moments and searching for missed signs, when what we truly need is grace, not blame.

Regardless of whether you are in the thick of grief and loss or are fortunate to have not been met with it just yet, gratitude is not just one of the most powerful tools you will have to combat the inevitable challenges of life, love and loss; it's a much kinder place for your soul to rest. Although it's never too late to adopt a daily practice of gratitude and reap its benefits, before experiencing significant grief and loss is the most ideal time to start implementing it. As humans, we are emotional beings who seek meaning and connection in life, and if we are honest, we are largely motivated by the ego, which tends to make everything in our lives, both what happens to us and what happens around us, feel so personal.

Taming the ego—whether in everyday interactions or in the bigger, life-altering moments that don't involve death—is a powerful and necessary practice. Absence and change are inevitable parts of life, and many of them feel like loss. But if we strip away the ego, we begin to see that not everything is as personal as it seems... not really.

We may not be able to silence the ego completely, but we can learn to quiet it. We can learn to meet life's changes with presence instead of projection, with compassion instead of control.

This analogy is a prime example of how our ego sabotages us in loss or absence: Imagine if my adult child, best friend or loved one calls me to say they got their dream job and so will be moving away. My ego may decide this impending absence (caused by distance) is a loss. Not just a loss but a personal one. I'M losing my friend/child/loved one. They are moving away from ME. Whilst the grief over the loss of closeness, proximity and even what you imagined this relationship would be like is both natural and common, it is ego-driven all the same.

If we are not careful, allowing our subconscious to make this about us could sabotage the relationship far more than any distance could. Making it about me diminishes my ability to celebrate the win with this loved one. Not to mention that perhaps any negative reaction or emotion of mine is more likely spawned from an abandonment wound I still carry (but may not be aware of), and one that if I'm not careful could negatively affect the relationship. If I decide, consciously or subconsciously, that this person moving away is personal to me and behave accordingly, I am not only likely to sabotage the relationship, but I also perpetuate my own suffering. It may lead me to have a negative narrative with them, similar to 'I can't believe you're leaving me' or 'but it's so far away, we will never see each other'. Not only does this subvert any potential celebratory conversations between the two of us, but it also facilitates a feeling of guilt on their part that could suppress any desire to share future wins with me.

What if, instead of reacting automatically, I paused and evaluated my emotional response? What if I allowed myself to sit with the feelings that arose–grief, sadness, maybe even fear–and met each one with compassion, not resistance?

There's a natural sense of loss, for instance, when your child begins to spread their wings. It's uncomfortable, yes, but also a sign that your role is evolving–as it should. That discomfort is part of the double-edged sword of doing a great job as a parent.

Because if we do it well–if we raise capable, confident, independent young adults–the inevitable result is that they'll go. They'll launch into a world full of unknowns, believing in themselves and their ability to navigate it. And while it can be bittersweet, it's also a massive win.

One moment, you're holding this fragile little being, unsure how you'll raise them into adulthood. Next, they're preparing to move out–maybe even far away–for a dream job they earned. You did that. You helped shape that dream-chasing, world-ready human. That's not just success. That's legacy.

Parenting might be one of the few things in life where the greatest wins can feel a little like loss. But that doesn't make them any less worth celebrating.

Absolutely. Allow your emotions. Sit with them. Validate the ones that need your attention. But then gently ask yourself, a*re some of these emotions more about me than they are about the other person?*

If I'm feeling abandoned, I need to pause and explore why. My loved one's success is not a rejection of me. Them moving for a job is not the same as them moving away from me. Emotional clarity often comes when we learn to separate the facts of a situation from the story our wounds or ego might be telling us.

When we begin to evaluate not just our feelings but the perception driving them, we start to reclaim agency. And when we acknowledge what's actually ours—like a past abandonment wound—we create space for healing. We might even seek support to process it. From that place, we can reframe the moment with gratitude rather than pain.

Gratitude truly transforms the lens. Suddenly, the list becomes endless:

I'm grateful I get to be their parent.
Grateful I raised a strong, capable adult chasing their dreams.
Grateful for a friendship that has meant so much.
Grateful I've been loved and have loved.
Grateful for the technology that keeps us connected across distance.
Grateful this isn't goodbye to life—just a shift in proximity.

It's not about denying sadness or pretending distance isn't hard. It's about ensuring the ego doesn't hijack the narrative and sabotage the relationship. We can express our feelings in ways that foster closeness, not diminish it.

Imagine saying, *I have to admit, my first reaction was sadness knowing I won't see you every day. But that's only because I love you so much—not because I'm not thrilled for you. I'm proud of you. I'm grateful we're in each other's lives. And I'll be cheering you on every step of the way.*

Gratitude makes space for duality. I can feel the ache of change and celebrate their joy. I can mourn what's shifting and give thanks for what remains. If I focus on the loss, I'll feed my pain. If I focus on what I'm grateful for, I'll expand my joy—and deepen my connection.

Denial and the Ego

Loss is a truth—whether or not my ego is willing to accept it. It exists, regardless of my resistance.

It is the denial of this truth that breeds unrest—and, at times, unbearable agony.

To agonise over reality as if it were still up for negotiation, simply because my mind can't fathom it, does not change the fact that it is.

Truth does not wait for our acceptance.

It is not softened by our disbelief.

No amount of effort, resistance, or longing can undo what is.

Loss is not made untrue by denial.

Our healing begins the moment we stop trying to rewrite reality.

But instead begin to meet it with compassion.

What Is Happiness?

What is happiness vs what it's not

I was recently asked how I would define happiness or what happiness meant to me. This got me thinking, and I came to the following conclusions.

I would prefer to start with what I think Happiness is NOT.

I don't think happiness is a state of being. I believe that we can all acknowledge that as women, we are hormonal creatures, and as such our state of being is ever-changing. And Men... whilst you may not have a menstrual cycle, I hate to be the one to break it to you. Whether it's your internal hormonal shifts or the pressures of your external environment, our state of being is also in constant flux. If we define happiness as a fixed state (of being) that we are meant to achieve and then somehow sustain in spite of said changes, we set ourselves up for an ongoing sense of failure.

This misconception, I believe, is at the heart of so much of our suffering around happiness.

We chase it endlessly, feeling like we never quite arrive— or if we do, we can't hold onto it. And so the pursuit itself becomes exhausting, disheartening, and ultimately unsatisfying.

What I believe happiness to be is a perception of our life in spite of our ever-changing states of being. Our ability to be present and to perceive ourselves as content or happy, even amidst emotional fluctuations, life's inevitable challenges, losses, and the grief that follows, is a far more sustainable and compassionate definition of happiness. It's not about avoiding hardship, but about cultivating a mindset that allows joy, meaning, and presence to coexist with it.

I would define myself as the happiest I've ever been, and on paper, that's almost inconceivable for some people. Although I always considered myself to be present and living consciously, I now realise that it was not only on a superficial level, but that I lived in a way that meant I was conscious of risk rather than living consciously. Consciously invested in avoiding risk and subsequent loss, and that this was not only impossible but also anxiety-inducing. My need for control over that which life has shown I actually don't have any, neither am I entitled to, lead to a presence that served anxiety and unrest rather than peace and contentment.

I now realise that it's in choosing our perception of the parts of our life we cannot control, combined with our capacity for radical acceptance of them, that facilitates a sense of happiness and contentment.

If I acknowledge that grief and sadness can, in fact, take up space and reside in the same parts of my heart and soul as do happiness, joy and contentment, and neither negates the validity or presence of the other, then of course I can find more happiness and peace than ever - even amongst the chaos that is grief. This is the essence of learning to live and grieve simultaneously. It's the acknowledgement that my grief does not discount, limit or prevent my capacity for happiness, joy or a rewarding life.

If we are honest about our suffering, we can come quite easily to the realisation that it is made worse by the act of wishing things were different. When we put time and energy into rehashing or revisiting the past in a way that feeds grief (by wishing things weren't so), we prolong suffering. Don't get me wrong... of course, we wish things were different, but energetically investing in the unrest that said 'wishing' facilitates will not appease your pain nor facilitate joy.

I appreciate that sometimes we need to sit with our sadness and validate our sense of loss. Sitting with sadness also gives you the opportunity to reflect on all the good that was ... all the things about what or who you lost that were positive and that ultimately make their absence feel as intense as it does. Grief is like a coin with heads or tails. Yes, on one side, there is sadness associated with the realisation of their unending absence, but on the other side, there is all the beauty that their presence in your life made way for and facilitated. In time, with as much energy put into gratitude for what was, more so than sadness for what isn't or will not be, allows us the joy of appreciating what we have had as we now learn how to live and grieve simultaneously.

You're allowed to be happy. You're allowed to smile, to laugh, to enjoy moments and have fun. This does not mean your heart doesn't feel the sadness of loss or the heaviness of their absence. It simply means that by way of gratitude, we have facilitated space in our hearts for both realities to reside simultaneously - neither taking away from the gravity and/or validity of the other.

Comparison is the thief of joy

A mistake I have commonly seen since losing Rylee is the instinct of others to minimise their trauma, sadness, grief or sense of loss in comparison to mine. When talking to me, whether about what I had been through or something completely different, when people would bring up something traumatic, grief or loss-related, they would quickly follow it up (almost apologetically) with 'Oh, but it doesn't compare with what you've been through!' Whilst I appreciate this would be done in an attempt not to appear insensitive to my suffering, I urge you to look deeper at our instinct to compare our suffering and sense of loss and in doing so, often minimise your own lived experience.

Please don't do this. **EVER.**

The compassion you seek to deliver results in your own self-neglect. My grief doesn't need validation. It simply is. The presence of yours does not disqualify the validity of mine. And vice versa.

Yes, a lot of what I've been through in my life is at times inconceivable for people. Especially the trauma, grief and unimaginable loss of my teenage daughter, BUT when you put your life experience next to someone else's in an attempt to share love, meaning, connection, empathy or even sympathy and then minimise yours because in some way you deem it to be less than or even incomparable, you invalidate your own life experience of suffering and inversely impact your capacity for healing, joy, happiness, contentment and connection.

Your pain is real. Your grief matters. Your story is worthy—without needing to compete with or shrink in the shadow of someone else's.

You see, your grief, loss, trauma, etc, is relative to your life journey and how you experience and perceive it. If the truest form of love someone had experienced in their whole life was from a relationship with/to a pet, eg, a dog... the sudden or unexpected loss of that pet may, for a time (whether brief and fleeting or prolonged), feel insurmountable. Why should the depth, reality or validity of their grief be minimised?

What about someone who lost their ability to pursue their life goals or dream career due to illness or injury? How is this loss of an animal, a dream or a career and the un-lived potential of less value in acknowledging than my daughter's un-lived potential secondary to her suicide?

Grief is not a competition. Pain cannot be ranked on a universal scale. Your experience is yours to live, to love, to grieve and to heal. What bridges loss to joy is not comparison—it's acknowledgment. It's allowing our emotions to exist and our grief to coexist alongside each others. It's validating our sorrow, without minimising it, dismissing it, or waiting for others to approve it.

By invalidating, minimising or denying our grief and suffering, we stay stuck in a reality where our capacity for joy and fulfilment is blocked by the inevitable resentment and negative emotions that have not been allowed to be. Allowing and experiencing our grief (without needing to compare it to that of others or have it validated by others) is what facilitates us learning to live and grieve simultaneously. And it is our ability to do this that opens up opportunities for joy, contentment, connection and happiness in our lives, in spite of our pain and suffering.

I truly believe it is important that in life we validate our emotions and allow them to be. Sitting with them and realising that - Good, bad or ugly, they just are. By allowing them to be and feeling them, we open ourselves up to being able to acknowledge them as something that good or bad this too shall pass.

P.S. There is no such thing as good or bad emotions, only what we do with them.

Once we acknowledge our emotions and allow them to be, it becomes a choice whether or not we stay in that place. This is the difference between whether or not we take on a victim role. Most of us assume a victim role or mentality without even realising we are doing it. Of course, it's important to acknowledge and allow our emotions, because the alternative of denying or suppressing them not only leads to unrest and diminishes your capacity for peace and joy, but it can also lead to illness and disease.

Once we have felt the emotion, acknowledged it and perhaps even validated it, it takes courage to own the fact that staying in that state of say anger, sadness, etc is a choice and one that will result in perhaps either rage and/or depressive symptoms, or inversely increased capacity for joy, peace and contentment, etc.

When sitting with our emotions in a way that allows self-compassion, we will also find that things are not always as they seem on the surface level. For example, what we initially experience as anger is more likely to be sadness or grief, and jealousy may be an opportunity for me to acknowledge a deeper discontent with my own efforts or lack thereof.

It is in having the courage to drop the emotional armour that our brains perceives as protection and in allowing ourselves to be vulnerable that we open ourselves up to some of the most beautifully therapeutic and healing experiences in life.

If we learn to welcome our emotions with kindness, empathy and curiosity, and sit with them, instead of needing to immediately judge them as good or bad, right or wrong, we open ourselves up to so many lessons in life, personal growth and the ability to experience a fuller more rewarding life.

There is no joy without sadness. No appreciation of sweet without tasting sour. It is knowing the sour that makes the sweet taste so sweet. No grief without love or appreciation. Let's face it… If you lose or go without something that meant little to nothing to you, you will be able to get on with life pretty unaffected by the loss.

However, if and when you lose something or someone that means the world to you, the grief can be unimaginable. Without appropriate words to do justice to the at times overwhelming and seemingly unsurvivable sense of agonising heartache and loss that comes with the absence of someone or something you loved with every fibre of your being.

The irony of life is you can't have one without the other. You can't love someone so selflessly and with such pure intention and intensity that you'd give up your life for them, but then walk away from the experience of their absence untouched by a grief as overwhelming as said love.

To experience a love like this means that, whether their absence is sudden and unexpected or comes with the privilege of warning and the opportunity to say goodbye, you never actually walk away from the experience of their absence. A sadness takes up residence at the base of your soul, and you carry this with you throughout your life. Whether or not you let that sadness take the wheel is another thing altogether. Grief is the echo of love. The deeper the love, the louder the silence they leave behind. To grieve so profoundly is not a sign of weakness—it's proof that you loved with your whole heart.

It starts as a heaviness you're convinced will crush you into oblivion, and that makes taking a single breath feel exhausting. Never mind getting through one day at a time. You question your ability to get through one minute at a time. Your world comes to a crashing halt as your brain tries to comprehend all of the unmet potential and un-lived experiences, along with all of (both yours and theirs) hopes, dreams and wishes for their years and life not lived - that will never be realised. The world has never spun so fast around you as you struggle with the most basic things like eating or sleeping. You feel like an alien on this planet who no longer speaks the native tongue, and as though you're dying a slow death of a broken heart... only to wake up tomorrow and do it all over again.

That was my experience anyway. And if you've experienced anything like this, please do not minimise the cause of such pain in an attempt to validate someone else's suffering.

Your pain is real, and your loss is valid! The good news is it's in leaning into grief, not running from it, that we begin to find peace. It's in saying yes to grief that joy, gratitude, and even purpose can begin to grow again—right alongside the pain.

The strength and courage it takes to get out of bed and face each day in those early days to months is beyond the comprehension of those fortunate to still be untouched by the gravity of such a loss. It gives you insight into why most (even temporarily) turn to drugs or alcohol in an attempt to survive, or perhaps simply to numb this previously unimaginable pain.

Back to why I believe comparison is the thief of joy though. We live in a time where technology and social media should mean we are more connected than ever. But somehow, we are seemingly more isolated and disconnected. Living a life through the lens of comparison, facilitated (more often than not) by the bullshit persona that social media allows, if not promotes. It is easy to appreciate how comparison in this instance is the thief of joy... whether it's comparing our lives, relationships, career choices, our bodies - to the carefully and at times manipulatively curated online representation of others... we all know someone negatively affected by said comparison.

Life is not a game to win. It's a journey to enjoy and make the most out of. Although I realise comparison statements were never said as an attempt at one-upmanship but rather an attempt to avoid offence or perceived insensitivity, I think we worry too much about saying the right or wrong thing.

When we compare our suffering or sense of loss and negative experiences to those of others and, in doing so, minimise it, we deny the validity of our lived experience and diminish the value of our life.

Your grief and sense of loss is yours. It does not lessen in value or impact because the details of it differ from mine. Our loss and the associated grief have the potential to facilitate joy and gratitude, and both are accessible to us at all times.

Our lived experience is directly impacted, if not governed by, our perception of it, and most live from a perception that has been formed, almost entirely, subconsciously as a result of childhood, culture, life experiences and beliefs that may in fact be outdated and no longer serving them.

When we start to assess our responses in and to life and evaluate our perceptions of life itself, ourselves, others and our lived experience, we are better positioned to determine whether our subconscious tendencies for perception actually serve us, or whether it's time we became more consciously aware of and responsible for how we choose to perceive said things.

It's not always easy to change our perception/s. It often takes courage and can be uncomfortable, but it's well worth it when you discover that your perspective isn't aligning with the kind of lived experience you truly desire.

So how can grief, loss, and sadness actually facilitate joy, happiness, or contentment?

I've said before that the grief we experience is directly proportionate to the depth of love or appreciation we've experienced. That means our sadness is not proof of brokenness—it's proof that we've loved deeply. When we reframe our grief through this lens, we open ourselves up to the possibility of revisiting that love from a place of gratitude.

Gratitude becomes the bridge. It doesn't deny the pain. It allows us to honour all the beauty that was—and still is—in what we've lost.

While we aren't always responsible for the thoughts that arise in our minds, we are responsible for what we do with them. If we feed our negative thoughts—ruminating, replaying, catastrophizing—our brains respond biochemically. We release the same stress hormones that deepen feelings like anger, anxiety, or sadness.

But if we pause and choose to feed thoughts of love, meaning, and gratitude instead, our brains respond differently. We create internal conditions that support connection, presence, and even joy—in spite of the pain. It's not about erasing grief. It's about choosing not to let it be the only thing we feel.

Similarly, if we want to feel good feelings, we need to feed and water positive thoughts, and a simple way of doing this is to flip the initial thought on its head. For example, if a thought pops into my head about how much I miss Rylee, I have a choice. To sit with sadness because perhaps it needs to be validated, but if I stay with and water those thoughts, they will subsequently lead to depressive symptoms.

Or I can shift the lens! I can think about how grateful I am to be her mum, to have shared my life with her and to have learnt so much as a result. I'm so grateful that, although she was only here for 15 years and gone without warning, that everything always came from a place of love and that the night before she died, I got to tell her how much she meant to me and that she hugged me for the longest time and told me how much she loved me. I'm extremely grateful for that experience and aware of how much harder life and grief would've been and would still be had I not shared that experience with her.

By feeding thoughts of gratitude, my brain responds at a neurochemical level in a way that promotes a more positive experience and reduces anxiety, stress and depression.

Gratitude has a tendency to cascade. Let's be real... anything we give our energy to will. Once I start, I could just keep writing about all the things I'm grateful for. When you create a tendency toward gratitude, you're asking your brain to look for good. The more it does it, the more it finds. It's like if you decide to buy a certain type of car, you suddenly see them everywhere. The brain will find that which it looks for. If your life experience tends to be a negative one, perhaps you have a tendency to look for negative things in order to validate the experience you're having. I'm not even suggesting you do this consciously. The good news is the brain can and will find plenty of examples to validate what your default setting is looking for, so if you desire a more positive experience, maybe it's as simple as resetting your default to seek out the positive through gratitude.

Gratitude leads to joy and facilitates a sense of happiness and contentment not previously experienced.

We can never outrun grief. And neither should we try. Understanding that it resides in and with us and that we don't always get a warning with regards to how and when it will rear its head, but that we do always have a choice how we perceive its presence, is invaluable if we are to create and facilitate a life worth living.

Victim mentality serves no one

Prior to losing Rylee, I thought I *wasn't* a victim in life. I know I certainly wasn't ever consciously choosing that role, but this journey so far has taught me about villains, victims, attachment, fear and ultimately love.

I see how minute this space we know as our life/world actually is in relation to what there is to experience and understand how naïve it is that we take almost everything so personally.

We think this room or environment you find yourself in right now is everything, and so we let it and those within it impact us so deeply and regularly ... we (more often than not) see everything as an insult or an assault. Labelling those around us as villains as a way of explaining or justifying these feelings.

For years, I would teach in my antenatal classes about the importance of owning your story and not giving your power away. Explaining that one of the ways we give our power away in life is by putting other people on a pedestal. We do this in pregnancy and childbirth, for instance, by assuming this person (Doctor, Nurse, Midwife) 'knows best and therefore will do best'. But this isn't the case. No one outside of you can know what is best when it comes to you and your life journey. Yes, they may have a knowledge base that differs from yours in a way that is extremely beneficial to you at this point in your life journey, but if we give our power away, we can inadvertently end up on someone else's agenda and unhappy with, if not traumatised by the outcome. You see, in order to put someone on a pedestal, you have to put yourself beneath them. It's easy to see by this example how we unintentionally give our power away in instances like this. I would encourage you to see taking on the victim role as just as potentially detrimental to your life journey. And it's not even something we do consciously.

But ... we do do it! We do it by labelling others the villain in our story. Although your villain story may seem valid and feel completely warranted. However, I urge you to consider that in order for there to be a villain, there needs to be a victim. So when you label someone in your story as the villain, it means that you (consciously or subconsciously) have assumed the role of the victim.

If you want the villain to lose its power, take responsibility for this and stop being the victim.

In my case, had I held onto the attachment of labelling the person bullying Rylee as the villain, or the person grooming her (which, believe me, would've been very easy to do), I would have, perhaps unknowingly, imprisoned myself in a state of perpetual victimhood, resentment and anger.

What I mean by that is if every time I spoke about her passing, I told it as a story of victim vs villain, I would have attached labels and, in doing so, given away my power. Whilst I appreciate and acknowledge the contributions of their actions to her passing and my subsequent grief, I chose forgiveness as a way of releasing myself from attachment to them as part of my story moving forward.

Attachment is our greatest source of suffering. It's a form of control or, at the very least, feeds on a need for or to control... circumstances, people, outcomes, etc. None of which are ultimately within our control. Not the way the ego wants you to believe they are anyway.

If we want to free ourselves from suffering, we need to let go of our attachment and instinct to control that which we ultimately don't. Had I stayed stuck in a place of attachment to them as the villains in my story, I would've closed myself off to everyone and, in doing so, lost so much more than just Rylee. Freedom from attachment results in a love not previously known or understood that takes up residence where fear once ruled... at the base of your soul. As a result, this love permeates everything you are and do.

When I speak about choosing forgiveness, it is often met with disbelief and statements like, *how could you though, I couldn't! I wouldn't be able to!* I think the thing is, we perceive forgiveness as something we are offering the perpetrator, but in reality, forgiveness holds such a more powerful and life-changing gift for the one offering it. Choosing forgiveness was not, in any way, about permitting behaviours or even saying things were ok. It was in no way allowing the perpetrator to remain a part of our lives. Nothing they did was okay, and this is likely the case in most situations where forgiveness is required. An inability to forgive keeps us standing in a doorway through which we are always looking back, wishing things had been different or that harm hadn't been caused. Staying stuck doesn't change the fact that it has though.

Forgiveness is the acknowledgement that I cannot change what is done, and continuing to look back, whether in anger, resentment or in wishing things weren't as they are, robs me of everything the present has to offer. It is an offering to self that allows us to turn around, out of that doorway and to see all of the beauty life still has to offer.

There is no shortage of unkind people in the world, but one blessing that forgiveness has facilitated for me is the realisation that there are so many more kind people. People in rooms I never would've entered had I stayed stuck in anger and resentment. Relationships I would've missed out on. Connection, love and friendship I would have lived without. Forgiveness was not easy to come by, but turned out to be one of the greatest acts of self-love I could offer my broken heart and damaged soul.

Genuine forgiveness frees you more than it could possibly free them as it is given without attachment. There is no attachment to how they receive it because it is given from a place of (self) love, but love all the same, which is free from attachment or a need to control the outcome. Therefore, when we love ourselves enough to release ourselves from the chains of unforgiveness, it is of no consequence to you how and where your forgiveness lands with the receiver. It frees you up to move forward with your life. To open yourself up to life and everything it has to offer, instead of being closed off and imprisoned by anger at the injustices.

There is a difference between accepting injustices, trauma, loss and grief as a part of your story and letting it define your story. It was around the one-year anniversary that I realised that we needed to be consciously invested in defining our life moving forward if we were to avoid unconsciously allowing victimhood. We made the conscious decision to acknowledge Rylee's death and everything that surrounded it as part of our journey, definitely an exclamation mark in our journey, but to not let it define it.

I spoke with the girls about how I wanted the next year to be *the year of who is Mia* and *the year of who is Zali*. When they asked what I meant, I explained that while Rylee's death would always be a massive exclamation mark in our story, I did not want it to define their childhood. I did not want them to become 'the Lower girls' or 'the girls whose sister took her life' but rather wanted them/us to spend the next year discovering themselves and in doing so start considering what they wanted to do with their life, who they wanted to be, how they wanted to show up in life, what they liked and disliked etc. The next year became a sort of self-discovery adventure where they got to step out from under the shadows of grief, and start to really take ownership over their lives. They started to learn how to live and grieve simultaneously, and that it was ok for love, joy and happiness to reside in the same space, and at the same time as sadness and grief, and that neither one need take away from the other, but instead exist paradoxically because of each other.

To this day, when people ask 'How are the girls doing?', it's interesting how often they expect a negative response from me about how poorly the girls must be doing. People look at you in disbelief when you say they are doing great or mention how well-adjusted they are in spite of their trauma and loss, as if they would be more comfortable and accepting of a negative outcome.

I don't take this personally, I just don't think people understand their power and so live out most of their life giving their power away in ways they don't even realise. It's human nature to look to place blame when things don't turn out the way we want or bad things happen to or around us. As if doing so would somehow appease the pain and discomfort of this newfound reality. But this is just another way we package up our power and give it away. It also only serves to perpetuate our suffering. It takes courage to hold onto your power; hell, it takes courage to even acknowledge your power to begin with. But with power comes great responsibility (wink wink)! It brings with it the responsibility of acknowledging that whilst so many things will happen to and around me in this life that I don't control, what I can and do control is how I respond to and perceive each of them.

The thought that two young teenage girls who have experienced unimaginable trauma would be well adjusted and in touch with themselves, their grief and each other is understandably a lot for others to comprehend. Especially when the story of their trauma in and of itself seems incomprehensible, not to mention occurring in an era that doesn't do well to foster our young people having emotional intelligence or an ability to be openly vulnerable with each other. But I am proud of the girls, who they are and how they show up in life!

I truly believe that everything in life is a lesson or a gift, sometimes both! And that you can use this perspective as a very powerful lens through which you view every part of and interaction in your life. I know Rylee was a gift (to me and so many others), who was here to teach me about love. The unconditional love a child has for their parent, self-love, the love a mother shares with a daughter, the love she showed up as in life, and the ways she softened the jagged edges of my soul that were damaged by so much trauma, I was convinced I was not equipped to parent girls. She did it so effortlessly too! Oh, how very wrong I was (about not being equipped) and how incredibly grateful I am to have had the privilege of loving her and being loved by her.

Knowing

From a deep yet unvisited knowing
that we are powerful beyond measure
comes an innate desire for more.

From ourselves, those around us and from life itself.
If our soul knows at its core that our limits are boundless,
then of course, it desires for more than a simply
mediocre life, love or existence.

Yet it's the unvisited that feels crazy making.

It's the UNrealisation of our greatness
that makes the yearning for more
feel unsettling rather than motivating.

It's the feeling that if I desire more,
to do more, be more, have more, give more,
experience more, love more, live more...

But I am unsure of the how-to or even doubt my capability,

that leads to a sense of failure or inadequacy

and makes us question our self-worth, our value,

our relationships and, sometimes, even our existence.

It's Okay To NOT Be Okay

I might be happy, but I'm not always okay

Please note that I am by no means suggesting that I, or anyone for that matter, can be immune to grief, or that by implementing the conscious and/or subconscious practices mentioned within you will stormproof your life from the seasonal changes of grief and its, at times, accompanying anxiety.

What I am suggesting is that it is possible to begin to exist within a beautifully positive reality where joy resides and peace is felt in increasing amounts, which also makes it that little bit easier to recognise the storms as temporary visitors and navigate them accordingly.

Understanding that whilst grief never actually leaves, in time the symptoms of it can enter and exit our reality as needed and do not need to become or remain an overbearing presence that completely steals our joy or our desire to continue living. If you feel this way or have trouble seeing even a glimmer of light at what feels like grief's never-ending dark tunnel, then please seek professional help in the form of counselling/therapy. If you are unsure where to start, then speaking with your GP for guidance, direction and/or referral is advised.

There are some incredible humans, well-trained in the art of helping people deal with situational crisis, grief, and loss along with the ongoing effects of loss. I have definitely sought help myself and will continue to do so as my life unfolds and undoubtedly continues to present me with its inevitable challenges.

As much as those around you may love and care for you, they are not necessarily equipped to help you through your darkest of days. Not in the ways you may need at least. And neither should we expect them to. It is, after all, not likely to be their area of expertise, and even if it was, they are likely too close to be of optimal benefit professionally.

No matter how strong a person we are, how much we have endured and how many times we've had to 'get back up' following the blows life has dealt us... There will be times when the only way to get back up is with help.

There are things that will happen in life that will have you feeling as though you could not possibly survive. I'm here to tell you that with the right people in your corner, you absolutely can! And yes! Your friends and loved ones will make up a good portion of those, but please see the value in seeking help (professionally) as often and for as long as you need throughout this journey we call life.

Growing up in poverty, I have been through child abuse (sexual, physical, psychological and emotional) and neglect, then drugged and date raped in my late teens, followed by a domestically violent relationship as a young adult, all prior to the horrifically violent and traumatic suicide of my teenage daughter. As a result, I have most definitely felt at times as though I could not possibly go on nor survive any further trauma. But I have. And I likely will… as I know that as long as we are still living, life is not done with us.

Whilst I don't expect more trauma like that of my younger years, I am in the second half of my life and know that this is just the beginning of loss yet to be experienced. With the ups come the downs, and some downs are so deep and so dark that they lead many to believe the only way out of the pain is death. At the time of writing this, according to the Australian Institute of Health and Welfare (in Australia), we lose 9 people EVERY DAY to suicide!

The darkness is real. But so is the light, and so many unfortunately do not access the help needed in order to find their way out of the darkness.

I think we are fortunate to be moving away from the once deeply ingrained stigma associated with admitting we are not okay or that we need help with our mental health. Whilst we are starting to value our emotional and mental health, we still have a long way to go. We can all agree that if I sustained physical trauma and had a limb that was hanging off, I would, without doubt access the emergency services necessary to stem the bleeding and not just provide life-saving measures but also continue with whatever care was necessary in order to heal the wound optimally and in a way that minimised the risk of ongoing complications in the future. I would also call the ambulance, which would take me to the Emergency Department, and then likely see both an Orthopaedic Surgeon and a Vascular Surgeon. I would not be driving myself to the GP, or waiting until I finished work, in order to seek help. Neither would I benefit from seeing an ear, nose and throat specialist if my leg were the issue. Similarly, I would see an oncologist for cancer, not an ophthalmologist (unless of course it involved my eye or optic nerve). But my point is, they are all Doctors. It doesn't mean their area of expertise pertains to your current needs.

I provide this analogy as an encouragement to take your mental health (and any situational crisis) as seriously as you would physical trauma. Just as you would select a treating physician based on the area of complaint, we should be unapologetic about seeking professional help from experts in the area of our loss or trauma. Just seeking a 'counsellor' is not likely to render you as much (potentially life-saving) assistance as seeking someone with a history of expertise and experience working within the area of which you are in need of support.

For instance, for us this was bereavement associated with suicide. In our case, I know firsthand how different this is. It is very different losing someone to an illness that potentially provides you with time, space and warning that you will soon be bereaved and so need to at least attempt to get some aspects or your life in order in anticipation of that loss along, with an opportunity to say goodbye to said loved one; as opposed to the sudden and unexpected suicide of a loved one that does not facilitate the same and after which there are and will forever be so many unanswered questions.

I am not comparing experiences of loss to say one is worse but rather stating that the way grief arrives in our lives can alter our immediate needs for help and that that help is best delivered by someone who has spent time in that particular arena.

The ways that I have processed my grief and trauma and been able to reach a place of relatively radical acceptance of her passing was no easy feat, and not something I could've achieved without professional help along the way.

There will still be days when grief is heavy, visits without warning, and my eyes leak the saddest of tears without my consent. Days when my smiley demeanour and positive vibe are clearly absent and those around notice. Should I try and deny its presence or hide my feelings, it only remains longer and feels worse. When those around ask if I'm okay I answer honestly. 'No... I'm not. Grief is a bitch' is usually all I can muster as tears stream involuntarily down my cheeks at the most inopportune time (like at the gym). But speaking my truth usually results in a much-needed hug where words aren't necessary, but love is felt.

Love is so much more powerful than words at this time. Owning our emotions and speaking our truth not only helps us decompress some of the pressure but also awakens in others a reminder of the value of their presence, giving them an opportunity to show up for us. Understanding that my emotions aren't bad, they just are and allowing me space to experience them without feeling the need to fix them for me is, in my opinion, one of the greatest ways a friend or loved one can show up for you. People want to help, but they often feel lost in not knowing how to, what to say and fear saying or doing the wrong thing, and so appear to do nothing.

Sometimes there just are no words—and that's okay!

People would say to me as time went by, 'I just didn't know what to say. So I stayed away. But I was always thinking of/praying for you.' I would encourage those around the bereaved to understand and be okay with the fact that sometimes loss leaves a gap for which there are no words capable of filling it, and for which the awkward silence felt by those who love and care for the bereaved need not be filled with sound or words but rather simply your presence and love.

While it's completely understandable to feel unsure of what to say to someone in the depths of grief, please don't let that uncertainty be the reason you distance yourself. You don't need the perfect words. In fact, there often aren't any. It is more than enough to say simply:

'There are no words… I'm so sorry for your loss.'

Those few words, spoken honestly and with presence, can mean everything. Silence and absence, however well-intentioned, often leave the grieving feeling even more isolated. Show up, even if you don't know what to say.

Your presence speaks volumes.

In our loss, we weren't looking for others to make us feel better, explain away our pain or provide some quote or phrase about how things happen for a reason or how they think I will end up working with the bullied because I lost a child to bullying. As well-intended as these are, I believe they stem from our instinct to fill silences rather than get comfortable sitting in/with them. It's the same societal pressure that makes it a cultural norm to comment on the weather when we have no interest in discussing it. We would rather say something than nothing, as nothing is too often perceived as rude or inconsiderate.

I can tell you in those early days it felt rude, inconsiderate, and like salt on an awful wound to hear phrases and speech I understand were intended to be the exact opposite. It is not the person's fault, nor was it ever said with malicious intent, but because I was good with my words and at expressing myself, people would repeatedly say (even in the very early days), 'God, you should speak in schools about bullying!?'

Overwhelmed I would think *FFS... She JUST died!*

I wouldn't respond. Hoping they would read the room and stop talking. But at the same time, my soul would scream, *Fuck off with your bullshit about me helping people! I've spent my whole life helping others. I don't even know how to help myself! I feel like I'm drowning, moments from death myself. I take a life-saving breath that only perpetuates my suffering by keeping me in this life! My soul is so fucking tired, and I don't even know how to survive. I'M NOT OKAY!*

For the longest time I would say to Ky, 'I'm still not convinced I can survive this!?' I would never hurt myself, but I felt, to the core, as though I was dying a slow death of a broken heart. I was convinced this new reality would become an intolerable norm and that, in my early forties, I would literally spend the rest of my days dying a slow death of a broken heart. Let me tell you it's an agonising consideration.

*I didn't get help in those early days in order to work out how to live a fulfilling life—**I got help to not die.***

People would frequently offer platitudes like 'one day at a time'. Let me tell you, it was one minute at a time. And each minute felt torturous, as if I'd slipped into some new reality where I was living in dog years. I felt 50 years older within a week. Taking a breath felt so fucking hard. My nervous system was so wrecked. I was on autopilot, taking such rapid, short breaths in a constant state of panic that made my body take a huge, deep sigh of a breath every 2 minutes. One where my body would almost gasp, grabbing its breath as deep as possible before returning to the all too familiar pattern of rapid, shallow breathing. This became a normal pattern of breathing for both Ky and I, and only one we would become aware of when someone else would notice the deep sighs and ask, 'Are you okay?'. It went on for the better part of a year. I had a tremor that became so normal I wouldn't notice until someone would say 'Your hands are shaking!'. Or when I would hug them, they would feel it (the shaking/tremor) in my chest and throughout my body and comment on it.

I had spent most of my life in fight or flight due to trauma and abuse, but nothing came close to the physical symptoms I can now reflect on that lingered long after witnessing

Rylee's sudden and unexpected death. I would relive her death every night as I struggled to sleep. Picturing myself running barefoot through the glass and throwing myself on my knees just trying to hold her hand before the police on scene pulled me away and the most heart-wrenching screams that left my body that night... the thought of which still brings me to immediate tears to this day.

There is no part of me that wants to present any of this as if I handled unthinkable grief with ease. Or that if you simply do A, B and C, your life will be wonderful and you'll be at peace. I have been to hell and back. Nothing about grief is easy. What it has been is a conscious journey, though. The thing about grief and trauma is it doesn't give you much of a choice. You either face consciously or you choose to numb it. And those that can't do either likely take their life. Personally, I found that only one of those was actually an option.

Numbing behaviours likely involve drugs, alcohol or other addictive behaviours, and I can tell you I understand completely why this would be the case. The courage it has taken to face it and walk back through the flames of grief, loss, trauma and complex PTSD daily is unimaginable. I have no judgement and so much compassion for those who choose to numb, and feel so much sadness and empathy for those who feel it too insufferable to remain in this life.

I acknowledge you for finding this book and promise that should you choose to face your pain consciously, leaning into it with the help of appropriately trained professionals, it is absolutely possible to learn how to live and grieve simultaneously, and in doing so, learn how to find beauty in life.

And in time, manage to love your new reality in spite of the sense of loss that overshadows it.

Please note that despite what we do, how positive our mindset or how significant our support systems in place might be, sometimes we need chemical help. Sometimes our ability to overcome depressive and/or anxiety-related symptoms is not a matter of changing behaviours or 'mind over matter', and we do need medication in order to help ourselves, our body and our mind. There should be no more shame in that than taking antibiotics for an infection or antihypertensive medication for high blood pressure. If we are not well physically, we take medication without hesitation, but then, when our mental health suffers, we feel we need to somehow 'fix it' without medication.

Taking care of your mental health is not a weakness—it's wisdom. Healing from grief, trauma, or mental health struggles isn't about strength. It's about support. The aforementioned chapters provide insights on how we can support ourselves rather than self-sabotage. This chapter is about knowing the limitations of our capacity for self-support and not having shame associated with needing to ask for or seek help. It's also about finding the right kind of care. It's about refusing to apologise for needing medicine, therapy, space, or rest. And above all, it's about knowing that your pain is valid–no matter how it compares to anyone else's.

Healing isn't linear. It's not neat. But it is possible. And the more we talk openly about it, the more we allow ourselves–and each other–to walk that path that is grief without shame.

Whilst jumping straight to medication as a first-line approach to the suffering associated with grief, loss, and trauma is unlikely to be ideal or necessary in most cases... sometimes it is absolutely necessary and something that can complement your journey if not help save your life. Having or finding a GP who has an interest and experience in mental health and managing complex grief will be very beneficial in not just helping with therapy referrals but managing possible medications if required.

I personally had to access supplements that helped calm and settle my nervous system as it ended up feeling like I was stuck in a car whose engine was being constantly revved. This was by prescription and under the guidance and management of a health professional. There are so many supports that go into creating a beautiful and rewarding life following great loss and when I reflect on my own journey I am so grateful for the people who banded around us making up the invaluable support network that held our heads above water in those early days when we couldn't and then continued to support us as we learned to swim in our newfound reality of the uncharted waters of grief and significant loss.

They say it takes a village to raise 1 child. I can tell you it takes a village to survive the loss of one!

Our supports since losing Rylee included friends, loved ones, acquaintances and even people we had never met who donated to the GoFundMe set up by a friend, or who provided us with temporary accommodation because we couldn't live where she had died. We were fortunate to have an amazing GP who continued to support us and who, without notice, would see us anytime without hesitation or fees. Counsellors and therapists who supported us in a variety of settings, from crisis services (who came out to the home in the early days), to group grief workshops for the girls, individual and relationship counselling, specialised bereavement counselling (again individually and as a couple) and equine therapy (the use of horses in grief counselling is awe inspiring). Complementary therapists like an Acupuncturist, a Massage Therapist, a Nutritionist, an Ayurvedic Therapist and a Personal Trainer. Most of these were people I knew or had previously cared for as a nurse who then reached out to offer their services as a way of helping. When I reflect on all of this and whether it was people who donated their time and services in the early days knowing I wasn't in a position to pay, or whether it was ongoing services I engaged, I realise now that each one made up such an incredibly valuable part of our safety net of survival and facilitated us not just surviving, but learning how to thrive. If any of you are reading this, I am forever grateful for you and the ways you made this life I now love possible!

I mention this because I want you to know *I am not special.* Yes, I'm emotionally intelligent and consciously invested in mine and my family's journey, but most importantly, I am supported. At times more than I realised. But it's our ability to acknowledge when we are not okay and in need of help and then accept said help, that enables those around us who desire to step up, the opportunity to do so.

It's okay to say no in grief

We recently had to navigate what should have been Rylee's 18th birthday. It has been 2.5 years since she died. The following is my journal entry from the lead-up to her birthday.

Rylee's birthday is two days away. She would've turned 18. It's a weird feeling. Hard to put into words. Almost as if every emotion possible was boiling just beneath the surface. But on the surface an almost numbness that disallows the processing of any of them. I feel exhausted. As if I need to sleep for a week.

At the same time, I appreciate this beautiful weather as I sit stuck in traffic moving at a snail's pace to get the coffee necessary to facilitate what's needed from me this day.

I love this weather, it's my favourite time of year. Not too hot or too cold. 22 degrees and not a cloud in the sky. I'm grateful the weather isn't miserable whilst my body needs to feel like this. It's the little wins as I navigate yet another missed milestone. Whilst I'm not interested in doing a deep dive into all the things I'm grateful for, I realise not only is this okay, but that it's not something that is necessary in order to still benefit from having gratitude as a daily instinctive practice.

Gratitude doesn't erase the pain of loss; it simply softens the edges of it so that you can continue to carry it with you in a way that doesn't cause the sharp edges of your grief to hurt others as you move through life without them.

Someone asked recently what we had planned for her birthday. I felt anger rise ever so slightly in me. There's not been many times I've felt angry at Rylee for what she did, and even when I have, it's quickly overshadowed by a deep sadness that my baby felt suicide was an option, let alone her only option. But in evaluating why I felt anger this time, I think it's the thought of this would-be major life event of turning 18 and everything it brings with it, being replaced with some alternative grief-related gesture which feels like it will only serve to exacerbate my suffering. I don't want to sit too long with all the things she would've, could've or perhaps should've been doing with her life had she been here to celebrate her 18th. And that's okay.

*It's okay to say no in grief. I'm not saying no to grief—**there is a difference.***

I'm finding my voice so that I don't find myself in situations that will only serve to intensify my suffering. It's days like these, when I'm not okay, when an outburst of the saddest heart wrenching tears lays in waiting just beneath the surface and who's presence, should they erupt, will seem an inappropriate response to whatever it was that appeared to have caused the upset—that I realize what an amazing job I'm doing of carrying my unimaginable grief with me everyday in a way that not only helps my girls learn how to navigate life, love and loss, but as we are doing so doesn't cause others unrest or discomfort.

It's days like this that I feel like I'm drowning in a sea of sadness, and where no matter which angle or direction I turn or look, I cannot find my way to the surface to facilitate a much-needed breath. These days aren't nearly as many or as often as they used to be. So instead of heading down a rabbit hole thinking about all the things that will never be or finding myself holding space for everyone else's grief as they attempt to 'celebrate' her birthday, I'm going to sit this one out.

It is so important that our grief and our ability to learn how to live and grieve simultaneously is a journey we are in some ways able to self-navigate. We didn't choose to experience the loss, nor did we consent to the grief. So, we don't get to choose or control the inevitable storms that will arrive at our doorstep as we continue through life. Some we can anticipate, others are sudden and unexpected. What we can do is choose how and with whom we navigate them.

I'm not suggesting isolating yourself unnecessarily. I'm saying don't put yourself in situations out of a sense of obligation for what we assume ours or others' grief should or needs to look like. I have let the girls know I don't wish to do anything myself, but that it doesn't mean they can't or shouldn't. They and their father want to, and neither they nor I are wrong for our choices. There is so much beauty in helping them understand that how I need my grief to look and feel should not determine their needs with regards to the same, and that they/we never need to apologise for any differences in how we choose to process, deal with or live with our grief as individuals.

Whilst I stand by everything I wrote in the aforementioned paragraphs, since writing it this morning, I have had a change of heart and I believe both sides of the coin are valid and worth mentioning:

Speaking with a friend who is in the thick of grief himself following the loss of his mother, I mentioned with tear-stained cheeks that her birthday was this week. This conversation offered me the opportunity to reframe this milestone. He said, 'So it's her 18th?!... and next year will be 19th and the year after 20th... they are all going to feel sad, and whilst the sadness is valid, it's about how you choose to spend that day. It may mean you buy the cake! Get an amazing cake and share it with your girls. Talk about Rylee and the beautiful memories you all share. Help those girls keep her memory alive. You are doing such an amazing job with those girls, they walk around the gym smiling and connecting with people! They are incredibly well-adjusted, thanks to you and how you show up, not just for them, but for yourself. Don't let the presence of sadness rob you of the opportunity to celebrate yourselves for how well you're doing and to celebrate that you had Rylee in your lives.'

Don't get me wrong, I wouldn't have changed my plans solely due to someone else's opinion of what would be right. But I happen to respect his outlook, and so have allowed myself the opportunity to reframe this week. In doing so, I was able to move from 'I just want this week to be over, I just want to get to the other side of it'... to a softer, kinder acknowledgement where I don't need to punish myself by disallowing joy because of the presence of sadness.

It is, after all, what I teach... That we get to choose our perceptions in life. Whilst we agreed we didn't need or want a cake, we also discussed the fact that you find what you look for and so decided together to look for the positives and gifts (something wonderful always happens around milestones/anniversaries). If I perceive her birthday as a significant reminder of everything lost, then every year I will suffer more than I need to. If instead I choose to spend it in gratitude with those closest to me, I can facilitate joy and peace whilst acknowledging sadness.

The girls and their father chose to take flowers to Rylee's tree with her friends, and I still chose not to attend this, but we also decided to do something fun together once they had.

Saying yes to grief isn't a one-off event. It's something you do and will need to keep doing across the lifespan in order to be able to learn how to live and grieve simultaneously. It's our ability to have a fluidity in our approach to life that will make the ride a much more comfortable one.

My outlook that morning wasn't wrong; it just was. My outlook that afternoon wasn't right; it just was. My ability to allow life to unfold without the rigidity of judgement means I can change my mind and my plans as I need to without feeling bad for doing so. Grief will always bring you to uncharted waters, even if you feel you are familiar with loss, because each loss will differ in the way that grief will present itself in and throughout your life. The way grief affects each stage of our lives is likely to differ also, so remaining flexible and compassionate to ourselves as we learn, and at times relearn, how to navigate grief and loss is one kindest gifts you can offer yourself.

Remaining flexible in our approach not only to grief but to self, will allow you self-compassion as you continue to work out who you are and who you will be in this journey called grief. Let's be real self discovery is a lifelong journey.

Some days are fucked!

You don't see it coming.

Grief shows up uninvited … Reminding you that it never actually left. You were just fortunate enough to have experienced a period where it took a back seat. Grief initially feels as though you're drowning and will never survive. It turns from the feeling of impending death to exhausting survival. Then, with effort and unimaginable (yet completely doable) courage, it turns into living–a life where it's not just your head above water, but your shoulders. You're enjoying life as you learn that it is actually completely possible to live and grieve simultaneously and in a way that sees you thriving, not just surviving.

*Then **POW!** Grief feels all-consuming again.*

As if you're in a container that's filled almost to the top with water, and where you can't touch the bottom, and are struggling just to keep your mouth at the surface, trying to breathe. Tears spill involuntarily down your cheeks without regard for where you find yourself or how prepared those around you are for this uninvited visitor we call grief. Your mind scrambles as it searches for a way out of this all-consuming darkness, back to the familiar routine of living and grieving, navigating each day with confidence in your ability to do so.

Grief is a rollercoaster, but what I have realised is that these more challenging days are an opportunity for me to choose self-care, softness and compassion, knowing that this too shall pass. For me personally, there is typically a hormonal component that exacerbates my grief. Since losing Rylee, I would find that around ovulation (when my body could make a baby), I grieved her at what I can only explain to be a cellular level. I felt the loss and her subsequent absence to my core in a way words will never do it justice. I have always struggled with severe fluctuations in how I view my life around ovulation through to my period each month.

More recently, I connected with an Ayurvedic therapist who suggested the symptoms I was describing may be associated with PMDD, which, once I researched, I could 100% relate to. I ended up being connected with a nutritionist who was helping me balance my hormones and my nervous system, mostly by adjusting or reducing the inflammatory foods I was consuming. I mention this because I didn't have PMDD. I most certainly had symptoms of it, but they were due to hormonal imbalances I'd suffered most of my life that, it turns out, were actually quite simple to remedy. I no longer suffer for 2 weeks every month in the way I've described. My state of being is a lot more constant and stable. And the inevitable (albeit slight) and normal spikes in my hormones are short-lived. So when these days of darkness visit that used to be weeks, I have the self-compassion to know that whilst my physiology may be contributing to how heavy my grief feels in this moment ... it will pass.

In the meantime, I am kinder to myself, expecting less and nurturing more. I also don't self-isolate nor do I hide behind a fake smile, pretending everything is okay.

*My child died! I'm **NOT** okay! And that's okay.*

Letting those who care so deeply know that whilst I will be okay... right now I'm not, means they are equipped with the awareness that in this moment, you may require more from them than you usually do. More might just mean a hug that lingers, allowing your nervous system the opportunity to settle a little; it may mean help with kids, it may mean company, it may mean distance or silence, as our grief doesn't always require words but rather permission to take up space without judgement or the need to fix it.

It's not for me to define what support or *more* looks like for you I only mention all of this in order to validate that when we find ourselves in the all consuming darkness of grief it can be tempting to not want to negatively effect others by exposing them to it, BUT it is by pulling the curtain back and allowing those around us to understand (even just a little) of what we are dealing with that we facilitate the opportunity for the much needed connection that can help light up that dark space and help us find the doorway back to ourselves.

People want to help.

Yes, sometimes it is beneficial to spend some time alone, but I would urge you to consider did my time alone help me feel lighter and more capable of continuing forward, or did it make me feel isolated and more alone in my suffering.

This Journey Called Grief

I am not who I was yesterday, nor will I be the same person tomorrow.

Life changes us. Grief changes us

Whether we want to or not, we change as life continues to unfold around us.

Gratitude also changes us. Everything in life is a lesson or a gift ... sometimes both!

It's what we do with the lessons and gifts that life hands us—more often than not in the form of challenges, that determines who we evolve into.

Be intentionally involved in your evolution. Be consciously invested in making this one magical life worth it.

Say yes... To love, adventure, passion, opportunity.

Say yes... To doors that open.

You can always leave if the room isn't for you.

Say yes... To grief when loss inevitably visits.

Because grief will change you regardless.

Saying yes to it means you get to meet the version of you who had the courage to put the pieces of your broken heart back together in a way that lets the light in.

The version of you who understands that love, joy and peace absolutely can reside in the same parts of our heart and soul as do sadness and grief.

And that the presence of each does not negate the presence nor validity of the other but rather that they exist parodically because of each other.

It is in doing so that we refuse to be consumed by grief, but rather can learn how to live and grieve simultaneously.

Learning to live and grieve simultaneously

There needn't be a dichotomy of living and grieving–love, joy, peace, happiness and contentment can absolutely take up space in the same heart and soul as does sadness and grief, and they can live simultaneously–neither taking away from the other but rather existing paradoxically because of each other. It's about learning to thrive, not just survive. To live consciously and find joy, passion and purpose. It's about balancing finding things to look forward to and appreciating things that have passed, whilst doing your best to exist consciously in the present.

Saying yes to grief doesn't prolong sadness.

After all, how can you prolong something that in and of itself is likely to be everlasting? Instead, it allows the radical acceptance of what is and, in doing so, facilitates more joy in your life. Ongoing denial only serves to block joy, growth and progress, and although sadness and grief may in fact be everlasting, in time they needn't continue to sting with the same intensity.

As we work on accepting what is, we facilitate an element of healing that sees what initially feels like a life-threatening wound turn into a scar that will forever remain and take up space in our soul as a reminder of the love that was. A scar that we will carry with us everywhere we go for the rest of our lives, but one that needn't rob us of our ability to continue living in spite of their absence.

I was watching a movie recently where the widower (many years after losing his beloved wife) had met someone and was speaking to his sister in law about whether dating again all these years later was the wrong thing to do. The sister-in-law explained that his wife had loved him so entirely and authentically that she would absolutely want him to be happy again. He went on to say how it felt wrong, to which she responded by saying, 'You are using your pain to justify not living... it's time to start living again'.

Like I said before, grief is an absolute bitch and one that may easily convince you to live out your days in a sense of martyrdom to its existence.

If we are not careful, we can end up using our pain to justify not living.

We can end up feeling as though our happiness and joy is a betrayal of those who are no longer with us and that if I am happy, joyful, laughing etc that somehow this must mean I didn't love them or don't miss them as much as I do or think that I should because surely if I did, these things wouldn't be possible!

I'll never forget how quickly joy and humour were replaced with guilt and shame the first time I found myself laughing at something after losing Rylee. I felt as though laughter and joy weren't something I was allowed anymore.

How awful would it be if this were true? If the true trade off for love, joy and happiness was to experience only sadness and harrowing grief once they were gone. Who in their right mind would seek to love in life? There is no part of me that doubts Rylee's love for me (nor mine for her), so thinking that she would want me to remain so heavy in grief and sadness that every day would mean isolation and feeling like I'm drowning is ridiculous. I don't pretend to know what happens to our soul when we leave this life, but I have said since losing Rylee that whilst I consider her to be in the next room of life, there is no version of her life I would want on hold because I continue to hurt. I don't want her stuck or waiting for me.

You see, that is what love is. Wanting the best for the one you love. So, if you can offer that to someone outside of yourself and you know that person loved you back, why wouldn't the same apply to you? I don't believe for a second Rylee did this to hurt anyone. I think she just wanted her pain to end, and her underdeveloped teenage mind thought suicide was the only way out of that pain. Her intention was not to inflict a reality where her parents and siblings felt laughter, joy, peace, or happiness was a form of betraying her. She would've done anything to avoid hurting us and would never have intended for her death to cause the agony it did.

So if we want to honour love, we do it by learning how to say yes to grief, allowing it to take up space in our soul, but without allowing it to consume us. We do it by learning how to allow the same (if not more) space for living, loving and experiencing life in ways we would otherwise miss out on if we let our pain be the reason we close ourselves off and shut people out.

It doesn't need to be a matter of one or the other. Things like living, loving, laughter, passion and adventure don't remove, negate or invalidate grief, the sense of loss or its associated sadness. And if we don't demonise the latter but rather accept them as the reminders of a love so strong and powerful it left its mark, forever staining our soul we can allow that stain to morph from the initially overwhelmingly painful reminder it is into a beautiful recognition of a deep and profound love we continue to carry with us as we begin to understand what it means to live and grieve simultaneously.

Life had us living and loving; loss cannot be the reason we stop.

I have needed to make some difficult decisions in order to facilitate my own ability to live and grieve simultaneously. Decisions to let go of things and even relationships that cause anxiety, unrest, or exacerbate my grief. One of these I didn't see coming was my nursing career. Something I believed I would do until I died, and for which my capability to do so was only interrupted due to my trauma and loss. The thing is, when I would put my availability down for a shift, I would end up biting my nails so bad they would bleed. I wouldn't be able to sleep; I would hope ceaselessly that the agency would say they didn't need me. Then I wouldn't get the shift, and all that would've happened is I'd bitten my nails to the point where they are almost gone and missed out on sleep. I am no better off, and I needed to acknowledge this. I wanted so badly to still be capable, but at the same time had to acknowledge that with all the work I had done to achieve a relative sense of peace and contentment, this was the only area of my life still inciting such anxiety. I spent the last 12 months grieving what I had essentially allowed to become enmeshed as part of my perceived identity and something I thought I would do across the lifespan. It was only once I made the call officially to walk away from what wasn't serving me that I felt the overwhelming sense of peace and being in flow that comes from listening to your intuition.

Love Letters & The Afterlife

A love letter to my inner child

In the aftermath of losing Rylee, I was reading a book called 'The Way of the Fearless Writer Ancient Eastern Wisdom Flourishing Writing life' (B. Kempton, 2022), about navigating the first year of grief. It suggests writing a letter to your inner child (the deeper part of you that thought this would never happen) about what you are and have been experiencing. I thought I would share it.

Dear Child,

Oh, how I wish I could wrap my arms around you and never let you go. You have the biggest, kindest heart of anyone I know! I wish I could have protected you from so much in life. So many of the people you should have been able to trust have abused, neglected and betrayed you. But instead of it making you bitter and resentful, you have spawned a resilience that, although at times you feel is unfairly required of you (over and over), will be the very essence of what will see you through what is yet to come.

My darling heart... so much awaits you, it's hard for me to see through the tears as I write this to you. I know you see yourself as a delicate flower, and whilst you are in fact as beautiful as one, you are by no means delicate. You are fierce and courageous in the most beautiful way. You have the kindest, most generous heart, and your ability to always find something to be grateful for will be where your resilience will be born from.

There is a pain waiting for you. One you could not possibly imagine or comprehend, and the agonising pain of which will, for a period, feel hopelessly incurable. You will feel as though you are constantly drowning in the deepest ocean and dying a slow death of a broken heart.

But first you will know love... in its purest form. You will know pleasure, joy, excitement, adventure and pride that will rip your heart open in the kindest of ways and let you into life's inner circle where your soul will meet its match and know true love. She will be your baby, your daughter and your mini me. You will get to be her mum, her idol, her hero, her guide, her teacher... and her student. She will teach you as much about love as you teach her about life. You will let each other down, but not nearly as much or as often as you lift each other up. She will be a beautiful reflection of who you were before the world got its hands on you... And seeing that reflection will open you up to a world of self-ove, compassion and admiration you would not have otherwise known without the opportunity to (love and) be loved by her.

And then she will leave. You will feel as though you lost her. And in part, lost yourself for a while. But in time, and large part due to that resilience of yours, you will come to realise you didn't lose anything. Her season will have ended, and what will be left is the lessons of love she came to teach. It won't be easy... my god child, it will be the hardest thing you will ever face... but you WILL face it... with the same courage, kindness and integrity you've faced everything that came before!

The gravity of one's loss is relative to the love experienced, and as such, there is no easy way out or even through what is to come. It IS going to suck! And for what feels like an eternity. In an instant, that beautiful heart of yours will shatter into a million pieces. The world will spin faster than it ever has, whilst yours comes to a complete halt. You will question your ability to survive this pain for which there aren't sufficient words.

BUT YOU WILL... survive!

In fact, you will do better than survive. You will learn how to live and grieve simultaneously and, in doing so, thrive. You will learn how to put the pieces of your broken heart back together in a way that will allow you to love the good, bad and ugly that is life and see it as a privilege to be here... in this life. You will understand (more than ever) where your energy is best spent and on whom... and you will create a peaceful, balanced life that is seasoned with passion and adventure.

Oh, how I wish I could wrap my arms around you and never let go... I wish I could protect you from what is to come. But I can't. And even if I could, I'm not sure it would be worth it... for you to miss out on all the beauty and life spent loving her and being loved by her!!

So yes, it's going to hurt... like no pain you've ever known. But the privilege of being her mum is going to make your life worth living, and your courage to keep living after she is gone is going to be the very key that unlocks a life filled with so much more love, joy, pleasure, excitement, adventure and pride than you could've imagined. You will make her proud. But more importantly, you will make yourself proud!

I love you dearly, and although I AM sorry for all the pain life has dealt you... I am NOT sorry for the beautiful lessons in all of it.

X. Es

A love letter to my daughter Rylee on her 12th birthday

Digging through old emails, I found this letter I wrote to Rylee on her 12th birthday about life and how challenging it can be, even for adults. I wanted her to understand that we are all on this roller coaster we call life together. And that I am, and will always be, here to love and support her. Obviously, if you read it from that perspective, now knowing she took her life because of bullying, that she did not allow me the opportunity to unpack with her, it is absolutely heartbreaking. Instead, I ask you to read it as if it is to you... intended as a gentle reminder to be kinder and more compassionate to yourself, and to know that there is never anything in life that is actually so bad that it is worth taking your life.

1st May 2019

A letter to my daughter on her 12th birthday

Today I messed up! The details don't matter, and no one got hurt as a result... but I'm hurting. I did something in poor judgement that could come back to bite me. I lacked insight and didn't read a situation correctly, and am now paying the price physically and emotionally. My chest feels heavy, there is a lump in my throat, and I just want to climb under a doona and sob (not cry... sob!). I feel as though I'm drowning in a sea of regret, guilt, remorse and shame... and it's f@cked!

I feel so disappointed in myself... because I expected more... and I usually deliver. It feels as though it's the end of the world (IT ISN'T... I promise. It just feels that way in this moment). BUT like even the best feelings in life- this too shall pass.

Everything in life is a lesson or a gift (sometimes both), and I will learn from this and come out the other side stronger and wiser because of it.

But as I'm feeling this way, I'm reflecting on just how harsh these feelings are to us as teenagers. And I dread the times when life will hand you your lessons and you'll mess up... not because I dread you messing up or making poor choices.

You see, my love, we all mess up. It's how we learn. And it doesn't stop just because we become adults. The learning never stops. I dread it because I don't want your heart to hurt like this. I don't want you to feel so disappointed in yourself that you can't see the light. I don't want you to hold onto feelings of regret, remorse, guilt or shame. I want you to be able to acknowledge them and learn from them in a way that allows you to always move forward in life.

The problem is when you live from a place of integrity and authenticity and then stumble and fall (because you will) the fall feels all the more painful. Unfortunately, as a teen, I did not have someone to help back up and to guide me through my mistakes, I watered feelings of guilt and shame as if they were plants for me to grow big and strong, and carried them with me into my adult life. It has taken a lot of self-help, pain and vulnerability to get out from under them and find the freedom to truly be myself... and to learn to love and accept even the darkest corners of my soul unconditionally.

I'm a firm believer that if the idiosyncrasies of being who you are does not cause another harm or pain, then you should unapologetically do you!! Living in this way is extremely rewarding and fulfilling because you own who you are, the choices you make and the consequences. No one can use anything against you because you own your journey, learn from your mistakes and give back more than you take.

BUT life is a journey... and it's important you remember your parents are on that journey too. We are no different to you, we are just a little further down life's path. And no matter what age or life stage we are in, we are all arriving 'there' for the very first time; and so deserve the time, space and permission to continue to learn our lessons. Daddy and I have never had a 12 year old daughter before, and so whilst we may not always get it right, we promise to always do the very best we can with what we know and to continue to grow with you.

I realise as a parent it is not my 'job' to mould you into something, but rather my responsibility to help guide you as you discover for yourself who it is you want to be. And then facilitate your journey in a way that helps you arrive safely... Authentically, unapologetically you, capable of achieving your goals and reaching your true potential.

I am no longer responsible for you or for your choices... From here my love, who you are will be who you choose to be. I AM responsible for helping you work through the consequences of your choices so that you can come out the other side stronger because you had the strength, courage and vulnerability needed to face and own each one of them. And in doing so, you will gain the knowledge and acceptance that everything in life is indeed a lesson or a gift... sometimes both; and that nothing (good or bad) lasts forever. Don't get stuck in the moment. Move forward. Learn. And love yourself despite your mistakes. Truly own them and learn to laugh at yourself, because when you can, life is a shitload easier and more rewarding. I promise to always offer you unconditional love, honesty, and transparency, and to honour my authenticity, so that you may learn to honour yours.

I love you more than life itself and am so proud to be your mum!

Rylee and the butterflies

The week before Rylee passed, I was in Cairns in North Queensland with her younger sister Mia. We were up there on holiday and in the evening found ourselves at a night market. While we were walking around looking at the stuff there, I came across this blue Ulysses butterfly wing in a glass jar. I found myself standing in the corner of this market just staring at it for the longest time. It was so beautiful. The same thing happened on the second night. Almost in a trance, I again found myself standing there (like Gollum from Lord Of The Rings lol) holding this butterfly wing in a glass jar and feeling really drawn to buy it for Rylee. I didn't have a lot of money on me, and it wasn't cheap. So I didn't buy it.

Each night, three nights in a row, I found myself back at this market again. Standing like a weirdo in the corner of the market, holding this blue butterfly wing in a glass jar. Just staring at it and feeling so overwhelmed with this, it's hard to describe, just this pressure, this feeling of 'You need to buy this for Rylee'.

I knew she was going through something at the time, I just didn't know what. We didn't have any warning or insight into the actual struggles that she was going through. She was a seemingly future-oriented kid, academic excellence, the kindest kid you've ever met, who just seemed to be living her teenage life. Such a beautiful kid, with such a big heart.

I knew she was going through something because she had kind of withdrawn a little bit. Not significantly. Just enough for you to know something was up. It is crazy how well we can hide our pain, even from those closest to us.

On the third evening, I ended up buying this butterfly wing in a glass jar. When I got back from Cairns I left it in a gift box with a love letter to her on her bed. It said:

Rylee,

I bought this for you because I think it's a beautiful metaphor for your life. When you look at it, it's easy to notice how much space the wing takes up, how the glass not only contains the wing but also puts pressure on it at different parts. The glass is like the world and the butterfly wing is you. The world can feel like a tight, pressured place to exist, and in some environments, as you grow, you may feel or be made to feel as though you are too much.

But instead of focusing on the glass and the pressure it resembles, look now at the wing. Look how beautiful it is and how no matter how you turn the glass or from what angle you look at it, it's so beautiful! Look at the intricate beauty and power in its design. That's what I see when I look at you. You have a power in you that you are yet to acknowledge and get to know yourself. But it's there all the same. It's why the world can be an uncomfortable and sometimes cruel place to be. Because not everyone has this kind of greatness in them.

Some people are like grains of sand in and out of the glass or world without any real impact on it. Some are like small stones that scratch the surface with their existence, but few have the kind of greatness and beauty that means they take up space in this world as intrinsically as the Ulysses butterfly wing in a glass jar, but without damaging the world around it.

Having the courage to acknowledge and accept your greatness will make it easier to live with, because until you find your purpose, it can feel like a burden or something you need to deny in order for those around you to feel more comfortable. Don't dim your light to make others more comfortable. Just get good at being intentional with about where and who you choose to shine your light on.

I love you with all my heart!

X. Mum.

I left that on her bed on the Friday night, and six days later she was gone. All her beauty and magic snuffed out in an instant. Forever 15 and never again mine to hold.

I think it was about 48 hours after her death, the face of my Apple Watch changed to a blue butterfly. If you have an Apple Watch, you know you need to go into the watch app to change the face. I didn't know what was happening. I thought maybe this was some really weird coincidence and it was some new system update, something they were doing now, and everyone had their Apple face change without them logging into the app or doing it themselves. I thought maybe it was something that would just last a bit, and they would change again automatically. When seven days passed and it was still a butterfly, I thought maybe 14 or 30, but what ended up happening in the aftermath of her death was every time I would look at my Apple watch, it was a blue butterfly, a different butterfly every time, but always blue.

There were so many ways blue butterflies kept appearing where they didn't need to or perhaps didn't belong.

Although it's too many to list all within the confines of this chapter, I thought I would include some examples.

It started with my Apple Watch and then, in the days after, with cards sent to us. I'd worked for years in Special Care Nursery, which is one department of a hospital, but I had also been working more recently in the birth suite - completely different departments of the hospital. Both teams of staff sent us a card after she passed away that had one single blue butterfly on the front.

I appreciate that a butterfly is often used as a symbol of someone passing. When we would work in birth suite, if we knew that a baby was going to be deceased at or shortly after birth or had already passed in utero, we would put a butterfly on the door so that staff knew not to come in unless it was a hundred percent warranted and to limit the interactions and interruptions into that space because of the grief associated with that birth. For this reason, I knew that butterflies have an association with death, grief and so forth. I was not aware, however, of the spiritual connection butterflies (in particular Blue butterflies) have with the afterlife and the symbolic nature their presence represents, being associated with a loved one who has passed, watching over you.

Although it's moving to consider now, it doesn't mean people intentionally chose a card from all of the Hallmark cards on offer, thinking about the significance.

So, then fast forward to us looking for a house. We couldn't live where she had died, and so we had sold the apartment. We were house hunting and having trouble finding the right thing. At the same time, someone had gifted us a weekend at Gwinganna, a beautiful lifestyle retreat that facilitated yoga, meditation and equine therapy. I had said to Ky, 'We're going to go away and manifest the right thing, put it out of our minds, then come back and end up finding the right house because so far we haven't found it. We haven't found our fuck yes feeling when it comes to a house. If we push it or rush it, we're just going to end up settling.'

And so we went away. Gwinganna had these newly built premium suites, positioned on a hillside overlooking the Gold Coast, away from the other accommodation options. The staff were aware that we were still very early in our grief and so gave us one of these suites to give us space away from the rest of the people staying at the facility.

At that point, we thought that for the price point we were buying a house at, we would need to purchase something in need of work, and so would need to renovate and do it up. I really, really wanted a fireplace, but everything we'd looked at so far only had a little pot belly.

As we get into our suite upon check-in, Ky said, 'Look… look at this carpet. I really like this.' I responded with 'Yeah, this is sisal… this is the carpet we'll put in when we renovate.'

After a weekend spent in therapy with horses, meditation and massage surrounded by the beautiful Tallebudgera Valley, we left thinking, 'Why didn't we think about houses in this area?' So when we got back from that weekend, we started looking on realestate.com in the area of Tallebudgera.

We found a couple of houses to go and look at. Neither had open homes; we were just doing a drive-by. Ky then asked if we should just go the following day because he was tired. Keen (and feeling a sense of underlying urgency to go right then) I offered to make him a coffee so that we could go now. The two houses were in the same street. We leave, and as we drive into this street, we come across this property that has a big open house sign out the front. Ky says, 'Look…

an open home!' I said to him 'That's not what we're here for?' To which he responds, 'I know, but... we're here...?'

And so we drive to the end of the street and look at the other couple of houses that we were actually there to see. Turns out we weren't interested in either of them. The street was quite long and so as we were coming back out of the street we reach the beginning of the property with the open home. Turns out this property is 4,220 square meters. So it's quite a big block. But as you come from the other end of the street, as you hit the property, you see the house pretty quickly and at first it just looked like a brick home... a lot like the home we had previously renovated. And we thought, it's just like our old home. So we kept driving. As we did, we were saying 'Is this still the property...?' and then I asked, 'Is that a granny flat?'

Ky responded with 'Pull over!' And as we jump out of the car with our puppy in tow, he goes, 'Imagine if this is just how we accidentally found our home... !?'

As we get out, Ky encourages me to go and see inside, saying he will stay outside with the puppy. And so I walk in, but as I'm doing so, this huge butterfly (probably the biggest butterfly I think I've ever seen) just follows me along the garden path. Not 'flies near me'... follows me all the way along the driveway and garden path to the door. As I walk in, I'm greeted by the agent, who was so lovely, and in a chirpy and welcoming voice, she says, 'Hey, how are you going today?'

I immediately just felt the tears coming. I looked through these beautiful French doors to my left, and there is newly laid, brand new sisal carpet all over this giant living room. And the whole wall was almost covered by this beautiful, big brick fireplace. The whole house was freshly renovated and had new appliances that hadn't even been used. Not only was it renovated already, everything had been done in the style and palette I would've chosen.

As the tears started streaming down my face, the best I could manage was to stammer, 'We...we weren't even meant to be here!?' As I pointed back out to the street as if somehow she would know I meant it seemed like pure chance that the timing we had chosen for our drive by of the other two houses perfectly aligned with this open house window of just 30 minutes.

This house was everything we said we wanted. And it was fully renovated. The agent asked if I was okay, and so I began telling her about Rylee and why we were house hunting. I ended up out the back with her, talking to her about our story and what had happened. As Ky walked around the back (a butterfly following him), he saw the agent and me both crying. He says, 'Oh, for fuck's sake, don't show her all your cards!?'

Meanwhile, I'm thinking, 'HERE ARE ALL MY CARDS!' The agent is sitting there saying, 'This is 100% meant to be YOUR house!' Meanwhile, it starts to sink in... The reason we hadn't seen this property in our searches was likely that it was out of our price range. I just remember thinking, 'What if we can't afford it. This is just mean!?'

As it turns out, the lady who was selling had raised their blended family of nine children with her partner, who had more recently got sick and died quite quickly. And so she was in the thick of her grief and relative to it. The short of it is that she received a phone call about a family that came through, who had just loved the house, which was exactly what she had wanted. She wanted someone to love it the way that they had. It ended up being the perfect house.

It was everything we said we wanted, and we didn't even need to renovate it or touch it. Were were fortunate enough to be able to reach a middle ground on price, and so we bought the house. In the time between contract and settlement (because the house was unoccupied), we went back a couple of times to show different family members, and (knowing about Rylee and the butterflies), each time someone would ask, 'Did you notice the butterfly following you through the garden?'

Fast forward to settlement. The seller, who knew our story but had never met us, left a little ceramic angel on the bench and out of all of the cards that she could have picked in the whole world, left a card covered in blue butterflies saying that she hoped we enjoyed the house as much as they had and that it brought us peace in such a difficult time.

Things like this kept happening. For instance, Zali didn't want to go to counselling in the early days. She had asked me, 'Why do we have to keep talking about it!?' I explained that she didn't need to talk about Rylee or what had happened. That she could talk about how it feels to be heading into high school. She agreed to go, but didn't want to go in alone and asked me to come in with her. This was very early days. And as we're sitting on the couch she says 'Mum, look!' As her whole face softened and her little shoulders relaxed. I look to where she is pointing, and there are all these blue cutout butterflies up the wall next to her. Obviously, it was not just the butterflies but also the counsellor's ability to build rapport with her, but she ended up looking forward to those appointments after that.

It just kept happening. I appreciate and teach about the power of us as human beings and our life force being our energy, and how powerful we are at magnetising stuff into our conscious awareness because energy flows where our focus goes. Or that we often become more aware of things once we put our energy on them, and that if we decide for instance, to buy a Holden or a Mercedes, that's all we see. We suddenly see them everywhere, even though we hadn't noticed them before.

BUT I wasn't looking for butterflies. There was nothing about me that had any interest in butterflies. And I truly believe that whatever it was that made me buy this butterfly wing in the glass jar was what facilitated so much peace that subsequently came from these ongoing events in the aftermath of her death. I don't even really have words to do it justice.

As much as people enjoy hearing the story, it still kind of feels a little bit much, even as I would find myself telling it. I would be explaining away the unusual presence of butterflies in different environments and situations to people who would notice, but still from a relative sense of disbelief myself. And I'm sure that there are people who are more involved in and knowledgeable of the spiritual realm of our existence who would probably be reading this and feeling completely validated or thinking, '100% !.. I fully see all of the connections here!' And it makes sense to them, whereas to us, it was just overwhelming.

Like having the capacity to try and comprehend (on top of the trauma we were going through), the ability for my Apple watch to change to a blue butterfly when I didn't do anything. And these experiences just kept happening. They kept happening everywhere we went, anywhere we were apprehensive to go. We were sitting on the Broadwater while the kids were in the water for Zali's birthday, 3 months after losing Rylee, and Ky was saying, 'I'm just so fucking sad, Es... like I just... I don't know how I'm going to do this!?' And this giant butterfly came and just hovered around his head. He sat really still, and he said, 'Are you seeing this?' Still, it just hovered there by his head before floating down to sit on his arm for a ridiculous amount of time. Probably two to three minutes just sat on his arm while the two of us sat under this tree, just crying.

I've never been this close to a butterfly in my life. This is not more of something that was already happening. It was just crazy.

As I mentioned in the previous chapter, the girls had started a business (The Kindness Crew) as a way of processing their grief and had started it in an attempt to raise funds because they had said to me that they realize (since losing Rylee) that life is short and they wanted to travel but didn't want me to have to pay for them. With some of their proceeds they decided they wanted to go to Bali for Zali's 13th birthday.

So February 2024, we went to Bali. We went with a friend and her 17-year-old daughter, and everywhere we went, butterflies were there. By this stage, it's just part of our life. The girls and I just view it as we know that it's 'Rylee and the butterflies'.

But my friend's daughter said to me at one point, 'I've never seen so many butterflies in my life!?' I asked her, 'Do you know about Rylee and the butterflies?' She said, 'No?'. I proceeded to tell her and give her this long list of examples of all these ways that it had presented in our life since losing Rylee, including all the environments where you would not typically find butterflies.

She sat there with tears in her eyes, processing it in that environment where we'd already spent a good portion of time in Bali, but now really acknowledging how much she had noticed it since we had been there with them. Because it was so many and everywhere we went. Even right down to the ocean! We chartered a private boat, just for our little group, to take us out into the deep blue ocean. I'm talking about the dark, deep blue ocean, where I'm not getting in the water because that creeps me out. I'm just there to make sure my children don't drown. (I'm not the biggest fan of the ocean).

So I'm in the boat and the girls are snorkelling. As they get back in the boat, the Balinese gentleman asks for my camera as he says he wants to take a nice photo of the 3 of us (my girls and I). And as we sit together, this butterfly comes along, just floating in between us and hanging around our shoulders. And even the Balinese were like 'Wait...what? We are way out in the ocean right now!?'. When do you see a butterfly in the middle of the freaking ocean? And again, by this stage, my friend's daughter knew about Rylee and the butterflies, so whilst we were blown away, we also weren't surprised. Things like this keep happening throughout our two-week stay in Bali.

We got back from Bali, and I had gone to the cafe Rylee used to work at. There's a lovely gentleman, Frank, who owns it, who had given Rylee her first job and had since become a big part of our family, and so had been significantly impacted by the loss of Rylee. I would often go back throughout different parts of my grief. Sometimes, just to be close to somewhere she had been so loved and appreciated. Sometimes it was too much though, and I'd stay away for a bit.

After having such a beautifully healing and peaceful time in Bali, I went back to see Frank. I hadn't seen him for a while. He hugged me a bit longer that time and said, I feel like Rylee's letting go. I explained to him that the week after we got back from Bali, my Apple watch changed from a blue butterfly back to the Mickey Mouse face that it had been prior to losing her! Not to something else. Back to what it was. He asked, 'Do you feel like she's letting go?' And I said, 'Yeah, I do.' And he said, 'Does that make you sad?'

My response was 'Well, a little bit... but there's no version of her life that I would want on hold because I continue to hurt, and I've always thought of her as in the next room of life. So if I think of life like a game of Mario Brothers, I don't want you stuck on level two, darling - just because I'm in level one... go **win the game!**'

Ayahauasca and the afterlife

There's no version of her life I want on hold because I continue to hurt! Because I'll always hurt. So why should her existence be negatively impacted by that? And I talk about her existence because a part of what I believe that butterfly wing was supposed to facilitate was the connection it created around the one-year anniversary. Coming up to the first anniversary of her death, I was struggling. I was not okay.

I started having people around me who were both close to me and those removed, talking about their experiences of ayahuasca. For those like me who are ignorant about what ayahuasca is—it's a plant medicine from overseas that works like a hallucinogen, but to create a spiritual and potentially healing or enlightening experience. I had no idea about it before this time. Like I said, people in close proximity to me began talking about and sharing their experiences. They had mentioned things like how they thought it would be amazing for us at that point in our grief. I remember being fascinated by their stories but thinking... not me. I'm not going to the bush to take hallucinogens. I was just closed off to it. I had gone to Fiji and smoked pot there when I was younger, and had a terrible time that nearly saw me end up in hospital, feeling like I broke my brain. I remember thinking, 'I'm not going to the bush to do some hippie shit.'

Needless to say, I was very closed minded about it at that point. But the more stories that I heard and the closer proximity the people were to me intimately in my life, that came with these stories, the more it piqued my curiosity. They say that because it is such a spiritual experience that you need to be drawn or called to it. It's not something you can view the way I was viewing it. It's not like you go to the bush and just do drugs. If done right... It's a whole ceremonial process with spiritual guides and healers.

I then found myself talking to a group of friends who had all attended a ceremony at different times in their lives, and each had their own amazing experiences and stories. By this stage, I was thinking that I wanted to do it, that I felt drawn to it, but also that I was scared.

I asked a friend, would she do it with me? I wasn't keen to go do a one night ceremony as I didn't understand how you could finish it and just somehow feel okay to drive back. There was a two night event that would fall the week before the first anniversary of Rylee's death. My friend had said, 'Yeah, I think I'll do it.' I started reading about this event, which was about the duality of life and death, and as I did, everything about it spoke to me. At the end of the information I was reading about the upcoming ceremony, the one emoticon that was used was a blue butterfly. And I remember immediately feeling a shift and thinking, 'I'm doing this. I don't need anyone to hold my hand. I'm going, I'm one hundred percent in this'.

I found out later that, as it turns out that the person who had created the event had created it with me in mind, feeling that she had been spiritually led to create this event because of me. A close friend of mine had been with this guide at the time Rylee passed, and the guide had told my friend, 'Your friend should really do ayahuasca. But she has to find it in her own time. She has to be drawn to it; it can't be forced.'

Fast forward almost a year, and she said she had felt guided to create this event for me. When I went to book it, I found it was booked out. I reached out to my friend and told her. When my friend spoke to the guide, letting her know I wanted to attend and to please let me know if there were any cancellations, she ended up changing the venue to be able to accommodate me. What eventuated would prove to be one of the most amazing experiences of my life... I didn't need to be scared at all.

I don't by any means want to be seen to be promoting ayahuasca as I understand firsthand that it is, in fact, a plant medicine and something you don't just go and do, but rather need to feel called to. You also need to be very mindful of your own potential contraindications, and if you were to choose to do it, be very mindful to do your research, ensure you are making an informed decision and be wary of who you entrust your journey to. My intention in sharing is only to give weight to the experience of connection to the afterlife and the peace that resulted. As much as I saw this whole unfolding as super weird, I've learned to lean into it because it's too many things to be a coincidence and a ridiculous amount of butterflies. And I do wonder if our association with butterflies and grief or loss is meant to be. Perhaps more important than where they sit in the food chain is their potential to facilitate a connection that reaffirms our innermost awareness that there is more than just this life. *That there is an afterlife?*

Anyway, I went away and did this experience of ayahuasca and as scared as I was, I leaned into it, and the experience that I had was... I don't know if you'd call it God, Source, Rylee... whatever it was took me through the multiverse and showed me all of it in the most beautiful colour, put me at complete peace with her existence - not at peace with the trauma that I had experienced as far as her death; But a hundred percent at peace with her existence and showed me that just because I cease to breathe doesn't mean I cease to be. It showed how our ego thinks that this is life. This room we find ourselves in, the interactions we're having– that this is the sum of our life. But in reality, it showed me that this is a tiny blip in the multiverse of everything that there is to experience.

For years, when I was younger, I would fear death. I would fear it because I would look at the intensity of my lived experience and all that I am and think, 'How can I cease to be, just because my body does or just because I stop breathing!?' And I struggled with that. With the discomfort and torment that these thought processes facilitated.

So it was literally one of the best things I've ever done in my life. It's not something that I would go and seek out or do again by any means. And I now understand why people said you need to feel called to the experience. As much as I stressed and was scared about it in the lead-up, thinking 'How can you just go take (something that works like) a hallucinogen and then just drive home?' But the reality was that at the end of the ceremony, they played the drums, and you just came out of it. It absolutely was less of a drug and more of a medicine, and it was definitely a spiritual experience and one that put me at complete peace to be able to navigate that first anniversary from a place of love and peace. I came back from it changed completely. I came back filled with so much love and having had this healing experience that I wanted to translate to the girls and Ky. I wanted to bring that home with me. And I did. It changed the way I communicated. It changed the way I showed up in my life. It helped me not take everything so personally. And it definitely helped me stop fearing death and the insurmountable unknowns in life.

Perhaps you've been through something similar. Perhaps you will go through a loss in your life, and there will be a symbolic nature of connection that validates your experience or keeps you feeling connected to that person. None of it has made me sad. If anything, it has probably helped strengthen me to be able to do everything that has been necessary in order to become this person today. The version of me that is able to stand in the rubble of my life, a life that I no longer even recognise and begin to start putting the pieces of my shattered heart back together. Not in a way that has any semblance to my life before, but in a really beautiful way. In a way that I love dearly and am so very proud of.

I'm so grateful to still be here.

I speak in more detail about the experience of Ayahuasca on my podcast Why Mindset Matters Episode 7. The Afterlife–Rylee & The Butterflies available on major podcast platforms.

Complex Bereavement

A note on complex bereavement

Complex bereavement, otherwise referred to as complicated grief or prolonged grief disorder, is the inability to move forward from the event and significantly affects a person's ability to function in their daily life. It is now officially recognised as a mental health condition which allows for clinical diagnosis and treatment if symptoms persist for more than 12 months in adults (6 months for children/adolescents) and significantly disrupt life.

The Diagnostic and Statistical Manual of Mental Disorders, Fifth Ed, DSM-5 (American Psychiatric Association, 2013), defines prolonged grief disorder with the following criteria:

- The death of someone close to a person occurring at least 1 year prior for adults or 6 months prior for children and adolescents.

- The person continues to experience intense yearning or a preoccupation with the deceased, with thoughts or memories of the deceased person occurring most days.

- At least 3 of the following for at least 1 month that leads to distress or disability:

    - Indentity disruption

    - Disbelief about the death

    - Avoidance of reminders of the fact that the person is deceased

    - Intense emotional pain

    - Difficulty reintegrating into relationships and activities

    - Inability to experience a positive mood or emotional numbness

    - Loneliness

    - A sense that life is meaningless.

Grief is a natural, human response to loss—there's no denying that. But sometimes, the pain can feel unrelenting, all-consuming, or impossible to live with. I remember feeling like that. And even now, there are still moments when those overwhelming waves crash over me. That's part of grief—it comes in storms, often when you least expect it. But it's important to understand: there's a difference between those natural, turbulent waves of grief and the constant, immobilising weight of complex bereavement.

While grief ebbs and flows, complex grief can feel like being stuck in an emotional undertow—where the pain doesn't ease with time, and hope feels out of reach. If you or someone you love is experiencing this kind of ongoing suffering, please know: you're not alone—and you don't have to stay in that place! Support exists, and healing is possible with the right care.

Grief is deeply personal and far from linear. And while the pain of loss can feel unbearable in the beginning, for most people, over time, the intensity softens. Grief doesn't disappear, but with the right supports it can and should integrate into our lives in a way that becomes not only possible—but necessary—for healing.

However, in cases of complex bereavement, this natural softening doesn't happen. Even with time and therapeutic support, the pain may remain raw and unrelenting. Those experiencing complex grief often feel stuck—trapped in cycles of numbness, distress, or deep despair.

If this sounds like you or someone you love, please know: this is not something to endure in silence. Please seek help immediately.

Think of it like this:

If you had a broken bone in a cast, you'd expect the pain to gradually ease as the bone continues to heal. Sure, you might have flare-ups or unexpected pangs–but overall, improvement would be expected. If instead, the pain stayed the same–or worsened–you'd likely seek additional medical help without hesitation. Mental and emotional pain deserve that same level of care. Yet far too often, stigma or shame prevents people from seeking the support they need.

My hope for you is this:

That your grief is not too unkind. That you find your way back to yourself, slowly but surely. And if you cannot find your way back to yourself (because that version of you no longer exists), that you are able to rebuild yourself and your life in a way that allows you to discover joy again–not in spite of your grief, but alongside it. And if you find yourself stuck–trapped in the aftermath of loss–please access help because...

You are not broken.

You are not alone.

And with the right support, it is possible to learn to live and grieve simultaneously—and to be ever so proud of the capacity you found within yourself to do so.

Main Character Energy

Honouring my Main Character Energy

As I write this, I'm sitting in a beautiful café in Ubud, Bali. Earlier today, I stumbled upon a hidden spa nestled among the trees atop a hill–and had one of the best massages of my life. I came to Ubud alone, carving out this time and space to finish writing this book. I needed to step away from the obligations and distractions of everyday life. The very things I'd been using–if I'm honest–as justifiable excuses for the procrastination that, until now, had kept me from finishing what I know I'm meant to complete.

I mention my experience with ayahuasca elsewhere in these pages, but there's something I haven't yet shared.

At the onset of the ceremony, panic began to rise. It started with thoughts of 'I have no idea where I am, I have no idea how I got here!? I don't know if I'm supposed to feel like this....?' As fear gripped me, it caused me to resist, and as I did, I felt an intense wave of nausea come over me. When I stopped resisting and decided to go with it... the nausea subsided immediately. Again, the waves of fearful thoughts came, causing a rush of nausea, only for it to subside immediately with each moment I stopped resisting. Not keen on vomiting it didn't take me long to surrender and lean completely into the experience.

Later, I found myself standing on the balcony of the venue that was hosting us, looking out at the pine trees. We were quite high up and surrounded by the trees, glistening as the rain filtered through the newly darkened night sky. As I stood there, I found myself thinking, 'I have no idea where I am, I have no idea how I got here... but ALL IS WELL IN MY WORLD... And I want to feel this feeling on different continents all over the world... I want to see and appreciate all that life has to offer!' I had never felt that depth of peace, well-being, and safety in my entire life. Not once. And certainly not in the year following Rylee's passing.

Fast forward, and at the time of writing this, it's been just over 2.5 years since her death. Shortly after arriving in Ubud–this town I'd never been to before, alone for my self-made writer's retreat–I was walking the 1km from my accommodation to the centre of town, down dark backstreets I didn't know. And suddenly, the tears came.

But not from fear. From peace.

The same quiet voice returned:

*'I have no idea where I am. I have no idea how I got here... but **all is well in my world**.'*

As someone who grew up believing the world wasn't a safe place, who later became an emergency and ICU nurse and spent years witnessing the fragility of life—how quickly things can change—I wasn't exactly the adventurous type. Certainly not someone who dreamed of solo travel. I carried the belief, buried or not, that the worst-case scenario was always the most likely one.

But the truth is, we are often shaped more by the limits of our exposure than by reality.

When I worked in the aged care sector, the atrocious conditions gave me tunnel vision. I became convinced we're all destined to die frail, alone, neglected in a nursing home. I forgot that the majority of people live full, independent lives until the very end. Similarly, working in the Emergency Department had trained my nervous system to fear the unknown. The unfamiliar felt dangerous—simply because I hadn't experienced it.

And so I clung tightly to the areas of life I could control (or at least, believed I could). I was a reluctant traveller. And certainly not someone who would ever, under normal circumstances, find peace or joy in travelling alone.

However, something changed when the girls and I first arrived in Bali. That trip cracked something open in me. It showed me what's waiting for us—on the other side of the fear that keeps us from living. It planted the seed. And that seed grew into a desire to travel. Even alone.

When I booked this trip, I intended to join a group writer's retreat. When that fell through, my intention was to concede defeat and accept that I would lose the $1500 of non-refundable flights and deposits I had paid.

As time grew closer, something came up on instagram suggesting that you ask ChatGPT the following questions...

I want to uncover the masks I'm currently wearing, the roles I'm currently playing and the illusions I'm believing. Please guide me through this process by asking me ten reflective questions to help me recognise the stories I'm currently telling myself. Once I've answered the ten questions, please step into the role of my higher self and analyse my responses, identifying the top negative patterns present in my life and the top positive patterns I can embrace and grow. Be direct, truthful and tough love is welcome. Then provide daily affirmations to support my growth, actionable steps to change my behaviours and embody my highest, most authentic self. Lastly, send a message of encouragement from my higher self to celebrate how far I've come on my journey.

There were obviously ten questions, but included in its response, one of the questions asked was, 'What does my most authentic self crave that I've been denying or delaying?' To which I responded 'travel'.

ChatGPT provided the following actionable shifts to embody my higher self (talk about Main Character Energy!):

1. **Declare your arrival**

Begin showing up as if you are already the international best-selling author and speaker. Update your bio. Rewrite your intro. Embody her energy–now.

2. **Break the caretaker cycle**

Practice saying 'no' even when it feels uncomfortable. Let others carry themselves. You are not responsible for their healing.

3. **Build daily evidence of your greatness**

Every day, write down three actions or thoughts that reflect your greatness. Watch your brain begin to anchor new proof.

4. Plan a travel-based creative retreat

Give your soul the gift of one bold 'yes' to your authentic craving. Even if it's a weekend staycation—honour the desire to expand.

5. Speak the vision aloud

Start or end your day by saying out loud: 'I am a globally recognised author and coach. My work transforms lives. I am living my soul's mission fully.' Train your nervous system to feel at home in the vision.

Message of encouragement from your higher self:

Beloved, you have come so far.

You've walked through fire, and yet here you are—still choosing love, still daring to believe in something greater for yourself.

I am so proud of the way you listened to your soul, even when it whispered instead of screamed.

You are not broken—you are blooming. Your desires are not delusions; they are roadmaps.

Stop waiting for permission.

You are ready. You are capable. And you are chosen for this purpose. I'm not in the distance. I am you. And I've been here all along.

I saw No. 4 and thought–What on earth are you doing sitting here thinking about cancelling a trip out of fear, while also telling ChatGPT (and ultimately, your higher self) that you want to travel?! The trip was already booked. And finances? Honestly, not a valid excuse. I ended up finding incredible accommodation for the whole week for just $250! I was going... alone.

As the date crept closer, fear started creeping in too. Whispering from the dark corners of my mind: 'Just cancel. You can't go alone. What if something happens? What if the volcano erupts?'

FFS... I wasn't even staying near the volcano. (Yes, I did Google it–checked how far it was, the current alerts, all the things). But then it hit me: when your time is up, it's up. I'm not saying be reckless–but worrying about what ifs only steals from what is. It clutters the present moment with anxiety about things that might never happen.

So I stopped feeding fear. I stopped pouring energy into creating what I didn't want and redirected it toward what I did. I bought travel insurance. Took every precaution a solo female traveller should. And then–I went.

That's why the tears came that first evening. Because sitting there, in a foreign country, with a calm nervous system and a quiet, grounded sense that all is well in my world–that was one of the biggest wins of my life.

I'm so deeply grateful I had the courage to walk away from my nursing career. To be honest with myself about the fact that it had become the only part of my life still inciting anxiety. And then to grieve it. Because it wasn't just a job–it had become a huge part of my identity.

Too often, we confuse our roles with our identity–and in doing so, we shortchange ourselves.

Depending on when you're reading this, the next statement may feel more or less true–but I'll say it anyway:

We still live in a world that doesn't truly encourage or honour Main Character Energy. And that's a damn shame. Because this is your one wild, beautiful, heartbreakingly sacred life. You should be running toward your dreams like your soul is on fire. But most of us don't. And I believe it's because, without realising it, we surrender to the following:

We let the many hats we are meant to wear across the lifespan seep into or be misconstrued as our identity. For instance, my professional role as nurse, midwife, even author… are all just hats I wear. Some for longer than others, and some that will change shape and form over time, but hats (or roles) all the same.

They are not who I am. The same goes for parenting. Being their mother or father IS a role we fulfil - one of the many hats we will wear and yes, one we will wear across the lifespan, but also one that will be required to change shape and form as they grow and as they do, so do the boundaries and expectations of my role. For instance, your role for a baby or toddler differs greatly from what is required of you in their teen years and again as they become adults and possibly parents themselves. You're never going to stop being their parent, though.

However, if we let ourselves be defined as parent (mother/father), if we let it become our identity, the real tragedy is that we facilitate our own suffering when they no longer need the same things from us that have become so enmeshed in our self-image and in turn, our self-worth. It is why so many suffer empty nest syndrome - it's a negative experience imposed by the perceived loss of the child, control and who we know ourselves to be come the inevitable time they want or need to leave home. It is also the very opposite of Main Character Energy!

If we have done our job well... our child's ability to leave the nest confident in their own capacity to navigate life but still aware that they have us in their corner is evidence that we have succeeded in our role as the loving guide, mentor and protector that it means to be a parent.

To avoid collapsing into an identity built solely around roles—and instead embody Main Character Energy in a way that feels aligned, grounded, and powerful—people must make a conscious shift from attachment to roles toward connection with self.

One of the girls' teachers said to me yesterday that over the last 2.5yrs as he's gotten to know Mia (currently 16yrs old) his perception has changed. I should mention this man was Rylee's favourite teacher and someone she admired and cared for deeply, as he did her. He said to me 'I used to see Mia as 'Rylee's sister'...but now I see Rylee as her sister'. This profound statement was said amongst a myriad of positive things he was discussing about Mia's resilience and her incredibly kind spirit that shone so brightly in spite of her trauma, and how much he admired her for her strength and character. But this statement created a profound shift for me. It made me realise how grief so subtly, yet significantly, causes us to give up our main character potential in martyrdom to it.

I realised that without knowing it, we were living as those who lost Rylee, those who were surviving her or surviving in spite of the loss. Rylee was now the main character, and we were all just extras in her play - a play from which her scene had ended. Yet we were all just left there on stage, not knowing what was supposed to happen next, because we thought we were going to spend the play with her in it.

Imagine if partway through a movie they killed off the main character and all that was left were extras... unsure of what the rest of the plot should be because it turns out that in life, Main Character Energy means your role is not just the lead but also the director and producer! That movie is not making it to screen... not the big screen anyway.

I realised that instead of seeing myself as fortunate to be a part of Rylee's journey (don't get me wrong, I wholeheartedly am), I needed to start viewing her as fortunate to have been a part of ours. If her term here was always only ever to be 15 years, how fortunate was she to have been born into a family that truly saw her? That loved and appreciated her so deeply. How fortunate was this little soul to have been a part of my story... to have had ME as her mum. This is not said from ego but rather a newfound awareness of the power that comes from stepping into our Main Character Energy and in doing so starting to navigate our hero's journey back to ourselves.

Reclaiming our Main Character Energy

The way we reclaim our Main Character Energy is by remembering that our essence—who we truly are—exists beyond the roles we play.

Yes, we are mothers, fathers, caregivers, professionals, partners, creators... but underneath all of that, we are souls on a journey. Roles may shift, fade, expand, or end–but our beingness remains.

To truly live in flow, we must do three things:

1. Anchor into identity, not role

Start by asking: Who am I when no one needs anything from me? If all my roles were stripped away–if I wasn't a parent, a partner, a nurse, an achiever–who would remain? This inner knowing becomes your anchor. That's your main character–the constant amidst the change. When we live from that place, we stop clutching roles as if our worth depends on them. We begin expressing through them instead.

2. Live by core values, not circumstantial titles

Main Character Energy doesn't mean always being the loudest, boldest, most spotlighted person in the room. It means knowing what you stand for. Living according to your truth, your integrity, your purpose–even when no one is watching.

When you choose your values as your compass, your path feels aligned–even if it's winding, unconventional, or misunderstood by others. You become less reactive to what's happening around you and more responsive to what's calling within you.

3. Keep evolving—on purpose

Roles can be beautiful containers for growth, but the danger comes when we stay in them past their expiry date. Main Character Energy means being willing to evolve—even if and especially when the evolution is uncomfortable. It's the courage to release roles that no longer fit, and try on new ones—even when they feel unfamiliar or vulnerable at first. This could mean changing careers, travelling alone, creating art, saying no more often, grieving honestly, or setting boundaries with people who only know you in your past form.

It's about deciding, 'I am still writing my story—and I refuse to stop at chapter five.'

Main Character Energy is not performative. It's a quiet, steady reclaiming of your truth, your voice, your vision.

It's grieving what was, celebrating what is, and leaning boldly into what could be—knowing that at the centre of it all... You are whole, you are worthy, and you are already enough.

Grief's martyrdom trap

Grief is powerful. It strips you bare. It rearranges your life and identity in a single moment. And if you're not careful, it can also quietly steal your Main Character Energy–that sense of agency, purpose, and personal significance you're meant to carry in your own life.

In the wake of deep loss, many of us unintentionally slip into martyrdom. We stop living and start simply enduring. We shape our days around the pain, not the possibility. Our choices become small, our voices quiet, our needs secondary–often because we feel guilt for surviving, or we believe that any joy we experience dishonours the one we've lost.

And while that kind of self-sacrifice might feel noble, here's the truth: whilst it might feel initially like you did... you're not meant to die with the person you lost.

But martyrdom tricks us into thinking that fully living again makes us selfish. That reclaiming joy, purpose, or dreams means we've 'moved on' too fast or forgotten them. It whispers, 'Who am I to feel okay when they're gone?'

That's where we lose our Main Character Energy–the energy that says:

- My life still matters.

- My story is still unfolding.

- My desires, dreams, and voice are still worthy of being heard.

Grief is a chapter, not the whole story. A chapter that may permeate the rest of the story but doesn't need to dictate it. Reclaiming your Main Character Energy doesn't mean denying your pain. It means refusing to make pain your permanent identity. It means showing up—messily, courageously, and imperfectly—to your own life, not as a supporting role, but as the lead.

And it's not about being the loudest, happiest, most 'healed' person in the room. It's about choosing to live intentionally, even when your heart aches. It's about giving yourself permission to matter again.

Because healing doesn't mean forgetting. It means remembering who you are—and writing the rest of your life with power, gratitude, and grace.

Main Character Energy isn't just about being the lead role though. It's about being the producer and director of your own life story too.

Because here's the truth:

You can't fully embody Main Character Energy if you're still handing the pen to other people. If you're still waiting for someone else to validate your script.

Or if you're stuck on a stage someone else built, performing a version of your life that doesn't even feel like yours anymore.

The Lead lives the story.

But the Producer sets the vision.

The Director calls the shots.

The Writer decides what makes it into the next scene—and what gets cut.

If you're only focused on acting out the part people expect of you, you may end up with a well-rehearsed life that looks good on paper but feels completely out of alignment. Main Character energy in its truest form is about taking full creative ownership of your life.

So what does that actually look like?

- As the producer, you choose where your energy goes. You budget your time, your emotional capacity, where, how and to whom you say yes and/or no and do so with intention. You stop giving your spotlight to people who haven't earned it and start funding the parts of life that truly matter.

- As the director, you set the tone. You decide what stays in frame and what needs to be cut. You choose the energy, the pace, the angles–you decide what scenes get a close-up, and what moments don't even make the final edit.

- As the writer, you reframe the narrative. You don't erase the pain, but you choose what meaning it carries. You write plot twists with purpose, not pity. You tell the story in a way that honours where you've been bu doesn't limit where you can go.

This is your story. Your one wild, precious life.

Main Character Energy means being unapologetic about living it on purpose, not default. You don't owe anyone a performance of the past version of you. You owe yourself the kind of creative direction that lets your life feel like it belongs to you again.

So don't just play the part. **Run the show.**

About the Author

Eslana Lower is a resilience mindset and manifestation coach, podcast host, and inspirational speaker whose work empowers people to navigate grief, trauma, and life's challenges with courage and gratitude.

After the devastating loss of her 15-year-old daughter, Rylee, Eslana committed herself to transforming pain into purpose, teaching others how to live and grieve simultaneously while embracing joy, love, and resilience.

She is the author of *Resilience After Great Loss: Learning How To Live & Grieve Simultaneously* and co-author in the international bestselling book series Start Over: Turn Any Loss Into a Sensational Comeback alongside Sir Marco Robinson and many other amazing authors.

Through her podcast Why Mindset Matters, as well as her coaching programs and live events, she helps people break free from limiting narratives, reclaim their power, and step boldly into the next chapter of their lives.

She also leads the *Why Mindset Matters* online community on the Skool platform—a space where like-minded people come together to grow, connect, and support one another. Inside, members gain access to her online programs, courses, and workshops, including:

- *The 28-Day Manifest Like a Mofo Blueprint* - a practical step-by-step guide to jumpstart your manifestation journey.

- *The Full 6-Week Manifest Like a Mofo Program* - a deeper, transformational experience designed to shift your mindset and unlock abundance.

- *Why Mindset Matters in Childbearing* - an empowering antenatal workshop that prepares you for all possibilities during pregnancy, labor, and birth. You'll learn how to make informed decisions, provide informed consent every step of the way, and ultimately avoid unnecessary birth trauma. No matter where you live, who your care provider is, or how you plan to birth, this workshop offers invaluable tools for every expecting parent.

- *Resilience After Great Loss* - a compassionate workshop designed to help you find your footing, reclaim your strength, and begin the journey of rebuilding life after loss or trauma.

Eslana's mission is simple yet powerful: to show that even in the aftermath of unimaginable loss, it is possible not just to survive—but to thrive; and that you are 100% capable of manifesting a life you love!

You can find Eslana on:

- **Web:** www.whymindsetmatters.com

- **Instagram:** @eslanalower & @resiliencemindsetcoach

- **Facebook:** @eslanalower & @whymindsetmatters

- **Podcasts:** Skool, Apple, Spotify (and all other major podcast platforms) *Why Mindset Matters*

- **YouTube:** @resiliencemindsetcoach

- **Email:** resiliencemindsetcoach@gmail.com

Useful Contacts

- Believe In U (Online Therapy) believeinu.com.au

- Lifeline Australia (24hrs): 13 11 14 or text: 0477 13 11 44

- Health Direct: 1800 022 222 healthdirect.gov.au

- Beyond Blue (24hrs): 1300 224 636 beyondblue.org.au

- R U OK? ruok.org.au

- Suicide Callback Service: 1300 659 467

- Mensline Australia: 1300 78 99 78

- Kids Helpline: 1800 55 1800

References

American Psychiatric Association. (2013). Diagnostic and statistical manual of mental disorders (5th Ed.). Washington, DC : APA

Kempton, B. (2022). The Way of the Fearless Writer Ancient Eastern wisdom for a flourishing writing life. Piatkus

www.ingramcontent.com/pod-product-compliance
Lightning Source LLC
Chambersburg PA
CBHW020525080526
44583CB00013B/745